Wet Wet Wet

Wet Wet Wet
A SWEET LITTLE MYSTERY

BRIAN BEACOM

MAINSTREAM
PUBLISHING

EDINBURGH AND LONDON

Photographs © *The Evening Times*

First published in 1995 by

MAINSTREAM PUBLISHING

COMPANY (EDINBURGH) LTD

7 Albany Street

Edinburgh EH1 3UG

ISBN 1 85158 739 X

A catalogue record for this book is

available from the British Library

Printed and bound in Spain by

Artes Graficas Toledo S.A.

D.L.TO: 1121–1995

CONTENTS

*OPPOSITE Marti in
concert in Arran, 1992*

ACKNOWLEDGEMENTS

Thanks to Brenda Paterson, the best sub-editor in the land.

Also to Russell Kyle, features editor of *The Evening Times*, for putting up with me when

the pressure told, and to Ian Pattison, who continually reminded me of the bigger picture.

Thanks also to Rod Ramsay, Mark Goldinger, Willie Knox, Russel Blackstock,

Rikki Brown, Jim Sherry, Jakki Brambles, John Dingwall, Aidan Smith, David Belcher, Mick Martin,

Andrea Miller, Russell Leadbetter, Tim Stevens, Robert Fairburn, Derek Chalmers,

Nick Low, Tom Morton, Bill Mills and Push Posters of Clydebank.

PREFACE

As teenagers, Wet Wet Wet were individually unremarkable. They were each as shy, introverted and limited in their ambition as any other working-class Scottish youngster in a depressed area.

But what has to be explained is what lies behind the success of four young dead-end kids from Clydebank, a no-hope town near Glasgow, that has taken them to the dizzy heights of pop stardom – and given them longevity to survive in a business that crushes heroes as quickly as it creates them.

How could four YTS kids, possessing little more musical weight than a stack of old albums, come together to produce a pop-soul sound that was neither of their time nor their country?

The answer lies in the chemistry that was produced when the band came together. As the friendship allowed the personalities to develop, so too did the musical potential.

But that's not to say the Wets' tale is some idyllic rites-of-passage story where four friends find fame and glory and go on to set the world alight with their music. Sure enough, there has been a great deal of that. But along with the success has developed a perpetual frustration. They've attained a level of success – yet, each member of the band is still overwhelmingly frustrated at the response to their music. Instead of enjoying the satisfaction of being hailed as one of the world's best pop bands, the Wets would trade it all for the status of rock musicians.

There's a huge dichotomy within the band. On the one hand they feel they have the talent and musical ability to blow other acts out of the water. But they still remain their own worst critics, constantly pulling apart their own material.

Part of their frustration comes from their difficult working-class background, which axiomatically has provided for their success. They grew up struggling to survive, and now success is still something that *other* bands have achieved. They are in many ways typical of a Scottish success story. They can't quite accept they've made it.

And in the moments that they do allow the luxury of the realisation to seep into their souls, they're not always capable of dealing with it.

The Wets' tale is undoubtably a rags-to-riches story but it is also a clear example of how young talent, finding almost instant fame, deal with the problems of success.

They manage to enjoy a pop-star lifestyle, yet they fight to retain most of their working-class perspectives; they can be entertained by Elton and Joe Cocker, yet fly back to Glasgow to enjoy a drink in their local.

Sure enough, although the four friends have fought against becoming the monsters that showbiz often creates, there are times when they've failed. And one reason for this is the pressure that rests on a world-famous band and their families as they continue to live in their home town.

Glasgow is a city they love, but it's also a goldfish bowl, where their every move is watched by fans and critics alike. The pressure on the band's frontman, Marti Pellow, has been particularly acute.

As a young man he likes to enjoy the fruits of his success – but still manages to retain a private life. And his public image is not the only source of concern. He has to be able to deal with the constant temptation of film and theatre offers and yet remain faithful to his friends in the band. Loyalty has always been paramount to the Wets. For example, at the end of last year, the band were close to landing a major American TV deal, but a death in Marti's family meant the idea was scrapped.

The immediate plan for the band is to stay together and to beat the world. Although the Wets have produced five Top Ten albums, they strive to achieve the real success which they feel eludes them. They have fought for musical credibility. Having made the most of their teen appeal – and early marketing encouraged this – they are nevertheless aware that large sections of the public refuse to acknowledge them as a genuine musical talent. The Wets are struggling to reach the middle (aged) ground that's occupied by bands such as Simply Red or performers such as Sting and Phil Collins. Time will tell if they can reinvent themselves in the eyes of the record-buying public. What the Wets want is to have the kudos of George Michael – without, of course, the legal hassles.

Chapter One

Wet Behind the Ears

MARK McLACHLAN picked up the phone one night in 1980 and called his friend Lyndsay McAulay, who lived just round the corner. 'We've got this band together,' said Mark. 'There are the four of us, but we need a guitarist. What do you think?'

Lyndsay was already in a band, but Mark's outfit sounded promising. Tommy Cunningham he knew by reputation as a good drummer. Graeme Clark was a music nut, as serious as they come about forming a successful band. Neil Mitchell, Mark had explained, had played drums until Tommy had come along and was now converting to keyboards. Neil was the only unknown quantity for Lyndsay but if the rest of the boys vouched for him then that was enough. Lyndsay took the decision that was to make him the fifth Wet.

'We remembered Mark [Marti], this good-looking guy from school,' recalled Neil many years later. 'He used to hang about with the smokers and do impressions of Paul Young and Boy George. He was a New Romantic, had a side-parting dyed burgundy and all the girls loved him. Anyway, we called him up and asked if he wanted to have a go. He was a bit funny at first. He said, "What's this singing game?" We said, "Come on, have a laugh."'

Tommy laughed about the moment. 'And he did just that. He was rough, but he was a thousand times better than Neil could ever be.'

The five friends, Graeme, Tommy, Mark, Neil and Lyndsay, rehearsed in Graeme's mum's house. But they were so loud that the band were in one room while Mark was consigned to the kitchen. For the first year he sang to the gas cooker. 'It was 1980. We were about sixteen then,' said Tommy. 'The Glasgow bands around at the time were The Bluebells, Strawberry Switchblade and Altered Images. It was a very arty scene. We were in awe of it because we were so young.'

PREVIOUS PAGE
The young hopefuls,
1985

OPPOSITE
Marti Pellow, 1984

FOLLOWING PAGES
Graeme Clark, 1984,
Neil Mitchell, 1984,
Lyndsay McAulay (the
fifth Wet), 1984, Tommy
Cunningham, 1984

Seven years later, as Wet Wet Wet, they were the British pop scene's Best Newcomers. By 1994 they had the biggest-selling single in Europe. In 1995, with another number-one album under their belts, Q magazine was to describe them as 'Clydebank scruffs made good'. In fact, they made very good. But why them? There were hundreds of bands on the Glasgow scene around this time.

'Thieves, drug-dealers or deadbeats, that's how we would have ended up,' claimed Marti Pellow. He was describing the likely fate of the five unemployed teenage friends who grew up and joined the dole queue together in Clydebank. And he wasn't exaggerating. Individually, the band members would surely have sunk into the pit of depression which the town became in the 1980s. When Mark, Graeme, Tommy, Neil and Lyndsay were kids, however, life looked promising enough. Sure, there were the problems endemic in much of the West of Scotland – alcoholism, religious bigotry, and large families surviving on low wages. But in the 1960s, there was hope. Nearby Glasgow was beginning to shed its 'Mean City' image of razor gangs and crumbling tenements. And although Clydebank, a small shipyard town four miles from Glasgow, was hardly Brigadoon, there was a mood of optimism. In fact, it was a little boom town. At 8.15 each morning and one o'clock in the afternoon, every house could set its clocks by the ear-splitting sirens signalling the end of the shipyard shifts. The yards that built the *Queen Mary* and the *QEII* would go on producing great ships. And fathers would pass jobs to sons through the generations. Nothing was surer.

But that's not what happened. The early '70s saw a decline in heavy industry. Shipyard contracts slowed and factories started closing their *Marti Pellow, 1985* gates.

During the Wets' early years at school (Mark, Tommy, Neil and Graeme were together at the local Protestant primary while Lyndsay was at the Catholic school up the road), they were already sensing that the foundations of their small world were becoming increasingly shaky. They weren't any worse off than their friends – better off, in fact, because at least their dads were still earning money. But as they grew up, and saw around them money grow tighter and dole queues grow longer, they realised that any real future lay somewhere else, doing something different. All they had to do was figure out what.

Mark McLachlan, who was later to change his name to Marti Pellow, was born on 23 March 1965, the second of two sons. He was born under the Aries starsign, at a time when The Rolling Stones were at number one in the charts with 'The Last Time' and a Labour Government was in power. It was a time of new, mass-produced consumer comforts. Ordinary families were now buying televisions, fridges and Hillman Imps. Twiggy was the world's first supermodel, and the Biba-look and mini-skirts were in fashion. Mark's parents, John and Margaret McLachlan, had a typical Scottish working-class home in Clydebank. (Mark was later to adopt his mother's maiden name, Pellow, said to have Yugoslav origins.) Margaret had once been a club singer and had a dog called Elvis. John McLachlan didn't work in the yards; he was a bricklayer and he kept earning throughout the crisis years. Nevertheless, when the shipyards closed, the despair in the community affected everyone.

'Suddenly in the late '70s it was all gone,' Marti was to say later. 'There was nothing. The school gates were being thrown open and out came all these kids, but the factory gates were locked. You see what I'm saying? Men who used to get up at six o'clock to work now got up at eight to do nothing. And it totally affected my family. My father was a bricklayer who worked for Lawrence the Builders which was a predominantly Protestant firm. His father got him a job, no questions asked; but, when it came to my turn, my dad couldn't have got me in if he'd wanted to.'

Mark McLachlan, nicknamed 'Smiler' at school, found the best way of facing up to a bleak future was to play the joker. Linda Jain used to sit next to him in English class. 'He was an extrovert at school and a bit of a prankster in our class. Sometimes he got himself into trouble but he always had an impish grin ready, as if to say "Who, me, Miss?". He liked to play things for laughs. He was good fun and well liked, although the teachers probably thought he was a bit of a handful.'

But Linda said Mark wasn't one for the girls. 'They liked him but he seemed a bit shy when it came to females. Mind you, this was just fourth year.'

Tommy Cunningham recalled his first impressions of Mark. 'He was a show-off at school. He'd go round singing and doing impersonations of pop stars like Michael Jackson. He was funny. And he was very good.'

What Mark and the rest of the Wets weren't good at was schoolwork. 'You know how you get academically brilliant people who graft away?' he was to say later. 'We were not like that at all. You could say we were the clowns.'

Thomas Cunningham, far brighter than later school reports were to testify, was born on 22 June 1964. He lived a couple of miles up the road from the others, in Drumchapel, a housing estate built just after the war, with his parents, Tom and Isobel, and three sisters, Christine, Caroline and Isobel. 'I grew up surrounded by knickers hanging

23

everywhere,' he said, wryly. 'But my earliest memories about Drumchapel are just about being frightened of the place. Each street had a gang. From the age of five I remember being chased and walking round being very paranoid. But I had hundreds of friends.'

When Tommy was seven, his dad became a taxi-driver and he moved into a 'bought house' which, in working-class terms, gave the family a new-found respectability. He later told the story to Simon Garfield of *20/20* magazine: 'When we moved I lost most of my friends and had to start again. It was only a few miles further along the road, but when you're seven that's thousands of miles. I look back now and I realise I just became an idiot. I used to fight, but when we moved I just became a clown. A few people I know managed to be both crazy

The original Wet Wet Wet line-up with Lyndsay McAulay (second right)

and clever and work hard. But it wasn't for me. School had some 1,500 kids in it, so I did all the normal teenage things like smash a few

windows and play cards a lot.

'But I would say I was very comfortable compared to other people's stories I've heard. I had a bike when I wanted a bike. I never starved or anything like that. And I was treated quite softly, probably because I had three sisters. It's not like having five brothers fighting against each other.'

Tommy, in fact, considered his family a Drumchapel success story. 'From being a lorry-driver my dad became a taxi-driver and managed to get a bought house with a garden. I think that's success. I'm not saying he's perfectly happy but he's a damn sight better off, emotionally and financially, than most people from a similar background. He's a worker. Education – nil. But he could drive and he could fight and so he became successful. He doesn't think about the ozone layer. For him, his life was bringing up four kids and making sure we're okay. As far as I'm concerned, that's always what I was aiming for.'

But the depressed Clydebank economy of the late '70s was to force Tommy and the others to rethink their aims. 'There were a couple of deaths at the end of my street,' remembered Tommy. 'There was also a heavy drug problem. By the time I was fourteen I wanted to move to London but my parents wouldn't let me. That was a place of drug-pushers, loose women and black people. My parents were very frightened for me, especially about drink and drugs. Everyone in Glasgow knows how dangerous drink is, because everyone has an uncle or a grandfather who's an alcoholic. Everyone.'

Like most working-class teenagers in the West of Scotland with nothing to do, football was their main form of escape. It was the love of the game that brought young Mark McLachlan and Graeme Clark

together. Graeme was born on 15 April 1965. He had two brothers, John and Alan, and his mum, Jessie, was a Sunday-school teacher. Even from his early school years, Graeme was seen as an all-or-nothing type.

Mark and Graeme played in the same amateur football team when they were going into their teens. One Saturday, the pair were both substitutes and got talking in the van on the way to a game. Then on the way back, contracts were given out for the next season and everyone got one – apart from Mark and Graeme. 'We were sitting at the back feeling really hurt,' recalled Marti. 'I went home and cried my eyes out that night. I was inferior. But I guess, somehow, the rejection made us stronger as people. When we later started to get rejections from record companies, I was already well experienced.'

The passing years have perhaps coloured Marti's memories with more than a tint of melodrama, but the experience actually proved to be important for another reason. Graeme now channelled his football energies into music. 'I used to go and stay with my Grandpa down the road,' he remembered. 'He used to play the piano in cinemas before films had sound, so my earliest recollection is of him trying to teach me to play, although it never seemed to stick in my head.'

The early inspiration did stick more than he knew, however, and Graeme grew up an avid music fan, listening to the likes of Slade. But then came the punk revolution at the end of the '70s and it simply blew his mind. More importantly, it gave him the idea that anyone could form a band. 'I can remember chipping in with my brothers for a copy of Slade's "Cum On Feel the Noize" but I really liked punk,' he recalled. 'And then my brother took me to see a band called Johnny and the Self-Abusers.'

Johnny and his Abuser mates went on to become Simple Minds, and

PREVIOUS PAGE
Wet Wet Wet in their
home town, 1987

by now the idea of forming a band was firmly fixed in Graeme's mind. The first major concert he saw, at the age of thirteen, was The Ramones. Still at school, he dyed his hair green, had it cut into a mohican, and sought out soulmates. That's where Tommy entered the picture.

'I first met Tommy when I was fourteen,' Graeme remembered. 'He was in the year above me at school and we'd catch the same school bus. I knew he played drums and he had an earring so I knew he was pretty hip. I brought him up to my house because we only lived down the road from each other. I'd just bought a bass guitar that had only three strings on it with ten pounds I'd borrowed from my parents.'

Tommy, by this time, had also lost himself in music. As a kid he would pretend to play drums with his mum's knitting needles on the arm of the sofa to the beat of his first Gary Glitter record. But by the age of eleven he had his own drum kit. 'Someone at the social club was selling a drum kit for fifteen pounds and my father, on the spot, said "My boy wants one!",' recalled Tommy. 'That night, I came home from the Boys Brigade – in fact, I'd just been thrown out of the marching band – and I walked in the house and there was the drum kit. It was heaven.'

Tommy learned the drums quickly and his dad put him up to play the working men's clubs, performing Country & Western songs. 'I knew I wanted to be on stage but I couldn't be a frontman because you've got to be handsome and have a great voice,' he said later, smiling. 'But playing in pubs full of drunks when you're fourteen is very, very strange.'

Strange or not, it gave him the confidence to have a go at joining a young band that didn't play Hank Williams songs. With his new friend, Graeme, he did just that. And when one of the members left, his place was filled by his cousin, Neil Mitchell, a boy Graeme had known from school.

Neil Mitchell was born on 8 June 1965 in Helensburgh, a nice, sedate town about ten miles west of Clydebank. With his parents, David and Betty, he grew up in Clydebank alongside Graeme and Mark. Neil was born to be mild. He was the original quiet, shy boy who thought things through, but kept those thoughts to himself. The smallest member of the band at five foot five, he was the most unlikely pop star, and very unlike his mohicaned mate, Graeme.

Neil's teen years were as depressing as the rest of the Wets', however. 'The thing that kept me going was watching *Top of the Pops* and thinking we could do far better,' he recalled. 'I had actually started on a drum kit my mother had bought me – you know the situation: a small council house with a set of drums – it was a nightmare. But as soon as Tommy picked up the drumsticks, that was it. I was on to keyboards.'

Lyndsay McAulay was brought up in a council tower-block a couple of hundred yards away from the home of his friend, Mark McLachlan. The boys had been friends for years – in fact, Lyndsay knew Mark before the rest of the Wets. He too had found escape through music, playing guitar from an early age and moving on to bass.

It was now the late '70s and the friends took to practising in Graeme's mum's kitchen, playing a mixture of Clash songs or new wave material by people like Magazine, Squeeze or Elvis Costello. Neil tried to sing. 'We all had a go at singing,' he said. 'I sounded the best but there was no way I could have handled being a frontman.'

And that was exactly what the band, who were then called Dante and the Lobster, needed. Then Graeme remembered one boy from school who could sing. It was a boy he had played football with for Goldenhill Amateurs some years before, the other tearful one who had been rejected on the team bus.

And they practised hard. Mark – who changed his name to Marti 'because it rhymed with a nickname, "Smarty", and sounded more showbiz' – brought round his mum's record collection. Marti's mum, Margaret, was a big fan of strong melodies from her club days and her prized collection featured the likes of Burt Bacharach and Carole King.

The boys added them to their other influences. Where Tommy had been a Status Quo fan, Neil was into ABC and Sinatra, Graeme was a new wave punk, listening to The Clash, and Marti was into Al Green, Stevie Wonder, The Eagles and Little Feat. But more and more, the black American influence was to take over. 'We got together one night to see *Saturday Night Fever* and we all became soul brothers,' said Marti later. It's likely that Marti and his mates saw something of themselves in the Tony Manero character – a no-hoper paint-shop salesman who dreamed of escaping from his dull, dreary life to the bright lights. Ironically, Marti was later to become a painter and decorator – and fantasise about stardom while singing into his paintbrush.

Music was becoming more and more of a necessary distraction. 'At Clydebank High I was put in a class with people who were more interested in sniffing glue or trying to score a wee bit of skag,' said Marti. 'That affects you mentally and people become stand-offish if you want to do well. But I always wanted to learn. I thought I'd like to take in a wee bit of theatre, a bit of a museum, but that was kind of unheard of. They'd say, "How fucking homosexual can you be?"'

The attitude of his classmates must have really killed off Marti's enthusiasm. But it didn't make a lot of difference, though, since they were all about to leave school and go on the dole – or try to make a real go of their music.

'If you come from Clydebank and you want to avoid unemployment, the only hope is to become a footballer, a snooker-player or a pop star,' said Tommy. 'We were shite at the first two.'

Scott Inglis was Tommy's teacher at Clydebank High. 'I remember he used to write poetry and he enjoyed reading out in class. There was something of a performer in him even then. But he wasn't into school-work. He used to say, "This will get you nowhere," but he really was a likable jack-the-lad.'

It was Scott who sanctioned their first school gig when the band, then in fourth year, were called Vortex Motion. 'The gig was a fund-raiser for the rugby club and the boys came and asked me if they could play. I said okay and they did a couple of numbers. They looked all dark and serious and the stuff was rough and pretty loud. I remember going to see them backstage afterwards and there they were smoking and snogging with girls from another school. Well, sometimes you just had to turn a blind eye. But it seems they had groupies even then.'

Scott Inglis remembers Lyndsay McAulay played at the school gig although he didn't attend Clydebank High. 'There was another boy in the band at the time and I recall him because the pupils always had to get special permission for strangers to come into the school.'

The school gig revealed how seriously the band took their music. Scott Inglis said they lived and breathed pop talk and only mixed with other kids with the same obsession. 'They were the music set,' said Scott. 'They weren't troublesome kids. Tommy, of course, was a year ahead, so he wasn't really part of it all. Neil, well, no one can really remember him – he was one of those kids who didn't cause a problem to a soul, so he didn't stand out.'

Marti and Graeme were different. Both seemed to be a talent looking for a stage to appear on, and it showed in their style. Modern Studies teacher Janet Sloan remembers Marti. 'Even then there was music in his head,' she said.

Marti was the Spandau Ballet–New Romantic fan and liked to look the part. Graeme was a green-haired punk, a Clash fan. It was the hair that eventually clashed with the headmaster's idea of school colours and effectively ended his schooldays. 'I know Graeme said he was expelled,' said Scott. 'But it was probably more like suspended.'

Marti's need to play the clown also caused a few upsets. 'I had to belt him,' said teacher George Roberts, 'because he was poking fun at one of the other boys in the class. But to be fair to him he just said, "Fair do's, sir, guilty," and took it like a man. I don't know if he's aware of it, but that was the end of corporal punishment in schools and he was probably the last boy in Scotland to be belted.'

Strange as it sounds, Marti had to adopt, at first, a low profile in the school. His older brother John's wild reputation – he was nicknamed 'Kojak' – went ahead of him. Marti didn't mix much with his brother at school, preferring to hang out with the music set. None of the band got stuck into the school-books, picking up only five O-grades between them. Not only did Marti not get a single one, but he actually got bottom grades in all five papers he sat. 'It was more a problem of attitude than ability,' reckoned Scott Inglis. 'In many ways we let them down by not having the facilities to develop their talent and keep them interested in school. Nowadays, that wouldn't happen. But the boys figured school was a waste of time. And music was their future.'

Chapter Two

Precious Times

BY THE time Marti, Graeme, Neil, Tommy and Lyndsay came to leave school in 1980–81, they could see themselves only as Dead End Kids. Neil couldn't find a proper job but filled his days driving for his father, a joiner. Tommy admits he also had a terrible time. 'I tried to get a job for a few months but there were four hundred people for every three or four places,' he recalled. Eventually, the young drummer boy gave in to the Job Creation Scheme and took up work making chairs. He lasted less than a year and then went on to work in a Chinese restaurant as a dishwasher. Things were desperate. 'I washed dishes at the weekends for a tenner,' he said. 'I did that for seven months. But I was at the end of my rope. I was just so frustrated, and if I hadn't found some way to express myself, I would have had a nervous breakdown. I'm not just saying that. I really mean it. I couldn't handle going out. I was a mess. I didn't have anything, I didn't have a job, any money, no girlfriend. I had holes in my shoes.'

Marti's mother, who of course had been a singer, supported her son's pop-star dreams. But her support occasionally weakened. He explained her dilemma. 'Other mothers would be saying to her, "Oh, my Brian has just finished his apprenticeship and he's got that car he wanted and he's engaged. What's your Mark doing?" And my mother says, "Well, Mark's been writing some great songs and that." And then she's hit with "So you're saying he's still unemployed?". And my ma would say, "Aye, but wait and see." But later I'd come in and she'd be a wee bit annoyed at me because obviously they're caring so much for you, and she'd say: "You've got a good song there, but look at the arse hanging out of your trousers, what are you going to do about that? Do you know the boy next door is getting married and he's got an Escort?"'

OPPOSITE
Tommy and Marti revisit
Clydebank, 1987

Marti's dad was a bit bewildered by it all. 'He would come in and say, "Have you been in the house all bloody day? I've been building a wall in the pissing rain. Get yourself a bloody job or I'll throw you out!"' Marti didn't want a proper job. But he went through the motions. 'Of course it wasn't what I wanted to do, but you can't suddenly say to your dad, "I'm going to be a rock star!" He'd have turned round and said, "Mark, have you been taking a hallucinogenic substance?" So I said I wanted to do as he did. I planned to ride it out for him because I love him.'

Riding it out meant going along with the YOP scheme and taking work in a sausage factory. He hated it. From there it was on to painting and decorating the homes of old people. He knew it offered little in the way of a future, but he genuinely liked the work and the rest of the guys. 'I remember working with this apprentice called Harry Weirdo,' he recalled. 'He had a little finger missing. A year ago I met the other apprentice and he had lost his little finger too. In fact, I almost lost mine when I was stoned. I slashed it with a camping knife, but the hospital managed to save it – otherwise we could have advertised as "The Clydebank Painting Co, just three guys with nine fingers, discount included".'

Marti enjoyed the decorating stint, but it brought problems too. He recalled one night in Drumchapel when he thought he was about to die. 'I was mugged there when I was sixteen,' he said later. 'I was doing a wee bit of work on the fly, painting an old biddy's kitchen. I came out of the house at 10.30 on a Sunday night; it was pissin' with rain and there were these guys lined up on the side of the road. You know when you get that feeling? You think, "I'm in for a spot of violence here." Anyway, five of them came up and kicked the shit out of me, took the fifteen quid I made for emulsioning the kitchen, took my leather jacket and they even swiped my braces. Broke my nose and all. You may wonder why I still smile all the time, because that kick certainly wiped the smile off my face that day.'

The attack was disturbing but not traumatic, for the Wets had grown up in a climate of aggression, much of it connected to football. Team allegiance in this part of the world was predetermined by religion. The Wets loved the game and are fervent Rangers fans but hate the religious divide that splits Glasgow into Celtic and Rangers, Catholic and Protestant. 'It starts off when you're very young with your best friend saying to you, "How come you got a Rangers strip for your Christmas?" – and he's wearing a Celtic strip. Then you start playing one-on-one football and you win and your friend will say, "Oh, fucking Rangers bastard." Things like that sort of build up as you grow older and grow away from him. And then it becomes a very taboo subject, occasionally flashing up in a bar. The tenements up the road from where I was born are almost totally Catholic. I used to go into bars and it was fine and no one really cared, but then towards the end of the night it emerges, that deep-rooted thing: "Oi, Billy Boy! Oi, Proddy!" You think, "Fucking hell!"'

On both sides of the religious divide there was the problem of survival. And religion had nothing to do with the sacrifice of a cow. Marti tells the story about how, when he was a young boy, he went up to someone's house to find them in the bathroom cutting a joint of meat from a whole cow. It was rustled outside Glasgow, brought home in a van and slaughtered in the bath, to be sold off.

If rustling cows was unusual, cars were literally the order of the day. 'You wake up in the morning and your motor's been done,' said

Tommy. 'I can understand that, though, because I've thought about doing motors in the past. I didn't actually do it, but it was a temptation.' And that's coming from the most sensible member of the band.

But it was becoming clear that if the boys didn't do something, *anything*, fast, they'd give in to that temptation. Music was the only reason they had for getting up in the morning. Music was the main thing on Marti's mind as he was painting the old people's houses. His favourite rooms to paint were the toilets because they gave his singing voice a great echo. At night, the five friends, who were now calling themselves Anna Hausen, would squeeze into Graeme's bedroom and listen to Elvis Costello or The Clash or an Otis Redding album which Marti had brought along. 'We were like brothers,' said Neil. 'It's a dream story – the five guys coming together and making a band.'

The band name was to change once more. Wet Wet Wet came from a line in a Scritti Politti song, 'Getting, Having and Holding', which said 'My face was wet, wet, with tears'. They added the third 'wet' because there were a lot of double-name bands around at the time like Duran Duran, The The and Talk Talk. The Wets went one better.

Then they decided it was time to make a demo. From Tommy's Chinese restaurant money and bits of cash the others had scraped together, they hired recording equipment to make that first demo. It was to be recorded in Tommy's house while his parents were off on holiday, but the tape jammed and they lost the recordings. But, with fifty pounds left, they went to a local studio and recorded three songs in two days.

PREVIOUS PAGE

Happy with the success of 'Wishing I Was Lucky',
1987

Derek Chalmers was the boss of City Centre Sound in Glasgow who engineered that first demo in 1983. 'I've still got the receipt,' said Derek. 'Eight and a half hours at four pounds an hour – thirty-four pounds. They were keen but pretty much like most of the young Glasgow bands. Tommy was still playing in club bands at the time and Graeme was pretty much the music brain. He was the one with the four-track studio at home. Marti was really just the voice although he had a real charisma about him. As for Neil, he was the least talented member, but I guess the rest persevered with him because he was one of them. What you could see was that those four were real pals together. But Lyndsay McAulay somehow didn't seem to fit in – although he was definitely a better bass-player than Graeme Clark.'

Finally, with that first demo made, Tommy began the assault on the London record companies. 'I looked out all my records,' he said, 'and found out all the major record company names and called up thirty of them, telling them about Wet Wet Wet and asking "Could we come and see you?". Three of them said yes, so Graeme and me went down to London and slept on friends' floors. Each day we'd go round the companies. Only three let us into their offices. Phonogram Records, who were to sign us two years later, said, "Keep trying, son. I really like it but there's a lot of competition out there." MCA said we were okay, but had a long way to go. At Rough Trade Records, a bloke named Geoff Travis said we were brilliant. But Geoff said most of their money was used up with a new band they had signed, The Smiths. He said as soon as The Smiths had a hit, Rough Trade would pay for us to do a record. About three months later, sure enough, we were watching *Top of the Pops* and there were The Smiths doing "This Charming Man". I rushed out and bought four copies so that it would be a hit and it would give Rough Trade the chance to work on us.'

Nothing was to happen with Geoff Travis. Nevertheless, the meeting had been crucial. 'He gave us hope. He was the first person outside the five guys in the band to show real interest.'

Geoff Travis regrets he didn't follow his gut reaction and immediately sign the Wets. 'I loved the demo and I thought Graeme and Tommy were really nice boys. Marti's voice on the tape was superb. But I wasn't in a strong financial position to take them on. I even offered the demo around to a few top producers but they declined. Still, I was keen. I came up to Glasgow to see them play in a club but by that time they had a manager and I felt he didn't really want to know me, so nothing happened.'

The man who had snatched up the Wets one night at the Night Moves club in Glasgow was Elliot Paul Davis. He had heard the Wets' four-track demo, and invited Graeme to appear at the Wednesday 'Open Night', when any band could go along and play.

Elliot Davis, a former trainee optician with an eye on the bigger things in life, was born in the south side of Glasgow. 'I won't say exactly where,' he said later in interviews. 'I don't want anyone to feel any pity.' Elliot was born into a Jewish family. His parents divorced when he was six, leaving his mother to bring up three children alone, until she later remarried when Elliot was thirteen. By the time his real father died, Elliot said he couldn't have cared less. Although he didn't come from a showbiz background, he had always dreamed of that lifestyle. And if he couldn't be centre stage, being in the wings was a close second. After Glasgow College of Technology, where he dropped out of his optician's course, he began calling himself Klark Kent and became one of the city's shoestring entrepreneurs, working in a record store, running a nightclub, a cassette label and a music fanzine. He turned to music management with a couple of white soul sisters named Sunset Gun who dropped him the day before they signed for CBS. Apparently, one of the girls in the band had fallen for a record company A&R man and the duo signed for his company. But a verbal contract in Scots law is valid and Elliot successfully sued. The money was to be later used as start-up cash for his own record label.

Even in the early days, Elliot had a reputation of a man who lives to win. Pop manager and club owner Mark Goldinger knew him back in 1982. 'The main thing about Elliot was his drive and love of money,' said Mark. 'He ran a band called The Wake and he was telling people they would have to pay £100,000 to sign them. It was a mix of self-belief and hype. Elliot used to phone me up and demand gigs and it was a form of commercial blackmail. If I didn't book them, he'd claim I'd regret it for the rest of my working life.

'Elliot was completely money-minded. I agreed to give him a percentage of the door takings on his band night and he stood at the top of the stairs all night with a little clicker in his hand, counting the number of people who came in the door. At the end of the night he began screaming we'd done him out of £12.50. His clicker count had included the free guests which, of course, all clubs have.'

Elliot's adopting the name Klark Kent suggests a man with a bookish image who sees himself as a bit of a Superman. But Elliot's alter ego, say adversaries in the music business, is far closer to Napoleon or Mussolini than Superman. A supreme organiser, a stickler for detail and a man for whom the term 'workaholic' could have been invented, he demands more than most from people around him. Clearly, if Elliot has ever read the book *How to Win Friends and*

Influence People, he quickly dismissed the sentiment. He was once described by Tom Morton in *Melody Maker* as a Woody Allen clone, 'a sort of Broadway Danny Rose on Irn Bru', but that description is false. Elliot is made of far stronger stuff. *Scotland on Sunday* feature writer Ajay Close didn't dislike him. But she found his fondness for keeping writers in their place hard to deal with. 'Just think of yourself as a Bullworker for his ego,' she said. Music writer Billy Sloan said Elliot wants to be seen as Brian Epstein, Col. Tom Parker and Berry Gordy rolled into one. 'I want to be Brian Epstein,' confirmed the man himself, referring to the infamous Beatles manager. 'I have the courage of knowing what makes good music and what makes talented artists. John Lennon once said, "If we knew what makes us successful, we'd give up tomorrow and all become managers." Well, I'd like to think I'd be the manager he wanted to be.'

This confidence and self-belief saw Elliot, a Celtic supporter, quickly earn the Wets' respect. He believed in them totally and talked immediately of chart/world domination. And so began a relationship that was to prove sometimes stormy, but ultimately successful. 'They were abysmal,' said Elliot, much later, about seeing the Wets in action for the first time in Night Moves – although, as one writer pointed out, *his* credentials were none too impressive either. Strange how the band's deficiencies are more pronounced in Elliot's hindsight.

Mark Goldinger saw the Wets play that same night. 'They were brilliant,' he recalls. 'I wish it had been me who'd signed them.'

Andrea Miller, now an executive producer with BBC2's *The Late Show*, was a music journalist and DJ at the time. And Elliot's girlfriend. 'The Wets came on stage and it was clear they had no real song structures, just choruses,' she recalled. 'But you could tell there was something really special about them. Elliot and I never had any doubts they would be hugely successful.'

In 1984 Elliot set up the Precious Organisation with Andrea Miller, based in a defunct police station in Glasgow's Maryhill district, using the Sunset Gun money as start-up capital. Precious was to be a Glasgow-based record label which would develop local talent like the Wets' and a couple of other hopeful groups. 'This was to be the Wets charm school,' said Elliot. Precious was named after a Dexy's Midnight Runners track, 'Let's Make This Precious'. The plan was to grow gradually, but before long it was a one-horse stable with the Wets the only band to go the distance.

Lyndsay McAulay was to fall at the first fence, at Christmas 1984, however. 'It just didn't work out,' says Lyndsay, now on the dole and still living in his Clydebank council flat.

Elliot elaborated. 'From the very early days, when we were recording demos in my bedsit flat in the south side of Glasgow, it quickly became apparent that Lyndsay couldn't cut the mustard. The boys and I discussed the situation and we felt we should ask him to leave. I felt I should be the one to tell him since I was the manager, but Marti insisted he do it, saying Lyndsay was their pal and that it should come from one of the band. To be honest, I didn't argue with him.'

Derek Chalmers' version of events showed the concerns weren't simply over Lyndsay's image. 'I remember Marti gushing to me at this time: "We've got this new bloke, Graeme Duffin, on guitar, and it's amazing," he said. "You just give him an idea and he plays it!"'

Derek had earlier said that Lyndsay's talent was clearly as a bass-player. However, since Graeme Clark was the founder of the band, Lyndsay could hardly have switched from six strings to four within the Wets.

But Lyndsay is today playing bass with a new band he has formed. His departure from the Wets, however, left him devastated. 'After I left the band it was a couple of years before I even thought about music again,' he said. 'I just didn't want to know. But nowadays I'm philosophical. There's no point in dwelling on it and I figured there were two ways to go: I could spend the rest of my life regretting it or I could move on. I chose to move on.

'And it was ten years ago; I've changed now. The rest of the boys have also changed. From what I've seen of what's been happening to the band, it all looks like one big pain in the arse. I look at them sometimes and I can see the problems they have. Of course, they have the money and that's terrific, and sure, I'd like some of that. But that's not what it's all about. I can honestly say I'm happy. I've got a girlfriend and I'm also playing in a band. Things are looking good. We've got a record deal and we're hoping for some big things.'

The band brought in Graeme Duffin as guitarist, on the advice of music writer Tom Morton, who had seen him play with Ricky Ross, later to lead Deacon Blue. Graeme, eight years older than the rest, was not to become a band member, but instead was employed as a session player. 'He's the fifth Wet,' said Marti, much later, referring to Graeme's growing role in the band, which has increased dramatically since *High on the Happy Side*.

Almost a year came and went as the band rehearsed constantly, guided by Elliot who, in the meantime, was mastering the art of hype.

'Elliot played the hype brilliantly,' recalled Derek Chalmers. 'People in the music business would call up asking to hear the Wets' demos but Elliot wouldn't let them, to help create mystery.'

Music journalist John Dingwall shared a flat in the south side of Glasgow with Elliot. He recalls how the band were instructed on interview technique by Andrea Miller. 'One of the key things Andrea got across to them was to mention the fact that they were unemployed. She and Elliot figured that would go down well with the London music press – four desperate teenagers seeking stardom etc. It worked.'

'I felt it was a case of less is more,' said Elliot, rewinding on the strategy. 'We were certainly élitist. I didn't want the boys to be playing pub gigs. No, I wanted them to play only high-profile gigs. And when they began to perform, I insisted every show be bigger than the previous one. In fact, the best shows were a handful of gigs we played at Glasgow University, in keeping with the notion of élitism. The band's friends, the Banky boys and girls, God love 'em, turned out in force every time – which all added to the hype.

'Playing universities meant good money and your name on posters. It gave you good credibility and, at this point, it was crucial. And it should be remembered that the students loved them. Mind you, Glasgow has always loved a soul band.'

It's hard to say how much of the Wets' elusive behaviour was shaped by Elliot at this time. John Dingwall told the story that Elliot never spoke to the band as a group. 'He'd arrange to speak to them individually,' he said. 'It was a question of power – divide and rule.'

Elliot disagrees. 'I only ever really spoke to Graeme during this period. It was his band and he was the only one I'd dealt with since the first time I saw them at Night Moves. Graeme was the one who sat down with a guitar and came up with the song structures. He was the driving force of the band.

'I'd call him most days to see how the boys were getting on with rehearsing and writing – and to see if they'd been out clubbing the night before instead of practising. On reflection, though, they were easily the hardest-working band I've ever come across.'

What the Wets didn't work hard at was their elocution. Elliot, it turns out, had coaxed the boys into attending voice classes to take the edge off their Glasgow accents. The plan failed miserably. 'You can shove your eloction lessons,' said the Wets after a couple of sessions of 'the rain in Spain', 'this is not for us.' Elliot didn't argue with the boys over this one.

By the end of 1984, no records had been released and the Wets hadn't been linked to a major label. Nevertheless, Elliot managed to swing a feature about Precious in *Melody Maker*. He talked about his organisation. 'Precious is 20 per cent my reputation and 80 per cent my ears,' he claimed. 'At present we have many options and we're examining them closely.'

By January 1985, the Wets still hadn't signed a record deal. But Andrea Miller in the *NME* waxed lyrical about the band: 'Although they are some way off chart-topping perfection, the potential of this inexperienced, unknown, shy band is frighteningly large.' Potential didn't pay the bills, however, and times were tough. Andrea said Precious and the Wets survived because they pulled together. 'We had all put our heart and soul into the band and we lived a hand-to-mouth existence. Sometimes it was soup-kitchen stuff, but there was always the belief the band would be big someday.'

OPPOSITE
On stage at the SECC
concert hall, 1988

It's difficult to understand how the band held together at this point. Apparently, Elliot and Andrea worked like maniacs to convince the Wets they had a musical future. Graeme and the others, meanwhile, lived off the dream. Of course, the boys had little else to look forward to. Their friends from Clydebank were on the dole – and had little hope for the future. The band had the sense to realise this.

But it was the worst of times. 'At one point Elliot rented a room near where he lived,' said John Dingwall, 'and then gave it to Graeme and Neil to rehearse in – and live in.'

John Dingwall, meanwhile, was writing for *Sounds* magazine at the time and hyping the band no end. 'Think of the late Marvin Pentz Gaye Jnr and the early Stevie Wonder,' wrote John. 'Think of a nineteen-year-old Clash fan with cheekbones like geometry, think of a future sex symbol of the '80s. Think of all these and you have Marti Pellow.' All this, before they had even recorded a note.

But at this time, Marti was in fact playing the shy card. 'I sometimes wonder why I'm trying to be a pop star,' he said at the time. 'My family are all building trade and dockyard people and suddenly I say, "Hey mum, I want to be a pop star!" It's hard for them to take, but I'm going to work and work really hard.'

In 1985 the band toured the country on the strength of the hype in the music press and the fan base they were gradually building up. The talent was now in evidence and the idea was to hook the big fish in the record companies. On 26 February, the 'young soul rebels' as Tommy had described the band, played a gig in Shotts prison on the outskirts of Glasgow. 'There were a few people in the audience I recognised,' joked Marti. But jokes aside, it was a wonderful marketing ploy to pull in A&R types and music journalists. It worked. Although Elliot crashed his car containing several A&R men – one was hurt quite badly – the Wets had hit paydirt. Suddenly, they rose from obscurity to become the subject of a record-company bidding war. It was even claimed, probably by Elliot, that presidential personages from record companies were flying from LA to the likes of Dundee to catch them play live.

'This was true,' said Mark Goldinger. 'They came to see the boys play at my club, Fat Sams, in Dundee. The A&R boys loved them, but they were especially keen on Marti. One bloke from Geffen Records said to me at the bar, "The rest of the band are shite but the singer's brilliant."'

One company tried to woo the band with a Japanese meal. It didn't work. 'For Scottish guys brought up on a diet of mince and potatoes, Japanese food is disgusting – all raw fish and ginger,' said Tommy.

Graeme talked to *Q* magazine about the attention the boys were receiving, the offers of flights on Lear jets and the lavish treatment in nightclubs. 'This attention was one of the best things that ever happened in our lives. The record companies were saying, "You're brilliant! You're brilliant!"'

Tommy, however, always the one to be calmer and more objective, was cautious. 'The main thing I remember is fear,' he said. 'I was shitting myself we were going to pick the wrong one. There we were, like a bunch of tramps, me trying to look good in my best three-year-old jeans, Giro in the back pocket.'

Gradually, record company interest developed. And the attempts continued to woo Marti away from his mates. One record company mogul took the singer aside for a pint of lager and told him he'd make him a solo star – if he ditched his three amigos. Marti left abruptly and told the others. That was one record company off the list. Another company boss phoned Elliot from the South Pacific and offered to 'help' Precious with £20,000. Elliot's answer was characteristic. 'That is a bribe,' he said. 'And then I told him he could stick it up his arse.'

Phonogram offered a £150,000 advance – not the biggest offer on the table – but the Wets had a good feeling about this company, which also had Scots bands Love and Money on its books. But football fan Elliot showed the studs as the deal was being completed, just to prove he could. When he negotiated the contract he added a clause that the company include a year's supply of Whiskas cat food with the deal. Why? It wasn't just the love of his four cats. 'I had to let them know that I was in charge,' he said. 'The cat food meant nothing. I could afford to buy it. But I was letting them know the Wets didn't come easily. You know, when we finally chose Phonogram, we recognised the deal wasn't as good as we could have got. But picking a company in the middle of the big league meant we could manipulate them more easily,' he later told the business editor of *The Glasgow Herald*.

In the April of that year the Wets signed a publishing deal with Chrysalis and played an all-important gig, at Glasgow University, in front of a group of record-company bigwigs. The concert went brilliantly, attracting good press. And on 22 May 1985, Whiskas and all, the Wets signed on the line. Two very turbulent years, for the Wets and Phonogram, were to pass, however, before any records were actually released. Phonogram, it was reported, spent £300,000 on them without a single piece of vinyl appearing, and it was said the record company were on the verge of dropping the young Scots.

The Wets by now also had a much less rosy view of the business partnership. 'As soon as you sign your name, you're scum,' Tommy said, rather emotively. It was a strong indication that the Wets and their record company bosses were to have a very difficult relationship.

Chapter Three

Wets Play Home and Away

NOW THAT Wet Wet Wet had signed on the bottom line, their Glasgow grit served them well when it came to dealing with their record company – although it's pretty certain Phonogram never saw it that way. The man who signed the Wets in 1985, Dave Bates, was delighted at the prospect of landing the band – until the deal was actually done. For it was to be two long years before the Wets released a record of any kind.

Tommy wasn't overly-impressed with simply being part of a signed band. 'I remember thinking, "Here I am, aged twenty-one, and all my friends from school think we've got a record deal and are making loads of money." And they'd be the ones getting a car and getting themselves set up in life, and we had nothing. The thing that kept me going, though, was the knowledge that all these friends wanted to do something else – they just never had the guts to try it.'

Andrea Miller said Elliot's influence at this point was crucial. 'A lot of bands get swallowed up by record companies and very often they are dropped unceremoniously. But Elliot fought to make sure the Wets were listened to,' she maintained.

Elliot agreed. 'Ninety per cent of bands would have split up in the period between signing in May 1985 and releasing a record in March 1987,' he said later. 'I was never given the respect for keeping the whole thing together, which I did. The Wets would be the first to admit it.'

But while the manager was getting the better of the record company, his ruling of the band was autocratic. He and the four Wets each had a 20 per cent stake in the band, so in theory all were equal and he could be voted down. But, at this point, he was totally in control. 'That was definitely the situation for the first couple of years,' he admitted later, 'but it wasn't healthy for either side.' Many times over the years he was to argue with the band over policy, more and more as their individual confidence – or stubbornness, as he would sometimes call it – grew.

Nevertheless, in 1985 Elliot saw his job as getting the best for the band. This meant not rushing them into anything, but allowing them to improve their performance and to write good songs. They were still rough and he knew it.

In June 1985 the Wets travelled to Amazon Studios in Liverpool to write and rewrite, many times over, songs such as 'Temptation', 'We Can Love' and 'Feel the Need'.

But problems began after they were assigned a producer. The band were happy at first to accept whoever they were given because they didn't, in truth, know what a producer actually did. They had heard of George Martin's partnership with The Beatles and Quincy Jones' work with Michael Jackson, but they didn't know that they would be giving away the final say as to how their music should sound. They only became aware of this when they heard the first 'produced' track – and hated it. Their gut reaction was that they, themselves, were the only ones who knew how their music should sound, and later events were to prove them right. But, for the moment, the Wets couldn't get studio bosses to trust their instincts. As a compromise, the boys flicked through some of their record sleeves and picked men whose names were linked to music they loved, names like Thom Bell (the Philadelphia Sound), Goffin and King ('60s sound) and Willie Mitchell (who created Al Green's sound).

Phonogram had a quiet laugh when some of these people were proposed as producers, claimed Q magazine. 'These were names who

Marti at rehearsals, singing 'Love is All Around'

hadn't troubled the charts for a decade or more,' they said. 'And instead the record company offered up John Ryan, who had a dance hit in '85 with "Obsession".'

'Ryan,' said Tommy, 'was a huge failure. Producers get a huge amount of money per track and he was accepting every first take. We paid him enough to buy a house and the result was rubbish.'

It was time for a break. In July the boys took their first real holiday. Marti went off to tour Europe, while Graeme and Neil went to the Greek islands. For the first time in their lives they had a few hundred quid in their pockets from their advance. One day on the beach Graeme got chatting to a girl from Paisley, Maureen Beacom (yes, sister!). He told her he was in a band and played her a demo of their songs. Sure enough, Maureen came home singing the praises of these two boys from Clydebank who were set to become pop stars. But she and the band were to wait some time before that potential was realised, because back in the studio, according to the *NME*, they 'went through producers like a man with flu goes through Kleenex'.

A further attempt with Phonogram producer Stephen Hague, the man responsible for OMD, also failed. 'More money and more time down the toilet,' claimed the Wets. 'All these guys failed us.'

Marti went even further. 'Most producers see the track as an extension of their penis, with "Oh, I think I'll go for a Duran Duran snare here",' said the singer, obviously embittered by the experience.

David Bates, understandably, was becoming irate. And relations with Elliot deteriorated. 'Elliot had been determined to prove he knew best and that I was well wide of the mark. True, I'd had two shots and missed. Things got so bad we couldn't say a civil word to one another, so I asked for another of our A&R men, Nick Angel, to take over from me. These days I find it hard to look the band straight in the eye because I'm thinking, "I signed you and I failed you." I feel guilty about what's happened and it's sad because they're very sweet guys.'

By June 1986, Phonogram were nearing the point of despair when, after dumping the two producers, the Wets finally got *their* man. They picked their idol, Willie Mitchell. He was the man who had produced Al Green, who had played for Elvis and worked with Tina Turner. But there was a problem; he hadn't produced anything for years and he was sixty. Phonogram, as you would expect, laughed in their faces. But the Glasgow boys won the day.

The Wets travelled to Memphis, their first visit to America and, apart from their recent break, practically their first time away from Glasgow. It was to be the most exciting experience of their lives. Memphis was a poor black city in the Deep South. Willie's studio, joked Marti, was said to run on coal. Their hotel was a social centre for pimps and whores. But the whole month was an incredible eye-opener.

The 'adorably gushing' Tommy, as he was described by feature writer Lesley Ann Jones, was astounded by the whole Memphis experience. 'Working with Willie was like working on Mars compared to back home,' he said. 'At his place it was open house, doors flung open to let the world in. Women would walk in with food for us – ribs, corn muffins, blueberry pie. Someone even flung her baby at Marti to hold while she carved.'

When the Wets and Willie met, everybody was nervous, but a few bottles of Jack Daniels solved that. They then told him what they wanted from him – well, sort of. 'We wanted to write about emotions

we had never really experienced,' admitted Marti. 'I mean, we were doing love songs, although we'd never been in love. Then Willie did this amazing thing. He just sat there for hours and told us stories about his experiences, about his life. He made it all sound so colourful we were able to pick up on it and use it as material for our songs.'

The Wets liked the sound Willie strived for, which was very much like a '60s recording. In fact, Marti used Al Green's microphone and

Willie maintained that the great man's saliva was still in there.

Tommy also raved about the experience – even though Willie told him to strip. 'I had always imagined I was a "feel" player,' he said, 'but when we were doing a song called "For You Are", Willie said I had to imagine a beautiful woman and get her in my mind. He said that to get me in the right mood I should take my clothes off. I said, "All right, I'll do it." He dimmed the lights down low and I got it in one take.' The story later became embellished to suggest Tommy played in his birthday suit; in fact, he kept on his boxers.

Marti also sang the praises of the producer after he tried to sing a song written by Willie and his friend, Ed Adam. Apparently, Marti was hitting the notes but not the heart. Willie taught him to sing as if the words were about himself – in fact, to be a good liar. Later Marti did the song and went into the control room and found the two old guys with tears running down their cheeks. 'That's why the Memphis Sessions mean so much to me,' he said.

Mitchell felt the same way. 'They're a number-one soul band,' said Willie.

It wasn't only the studio experience which left an indelible impression on the band's soul. This, after all, was a black town, steeped in black culture, the like of which the Wets had never seen. When the Glasgow boys walked into a nightclub the local band stopped and people stared. But it was all right, for word got round that these 'were Willie's boys from Scotland, England'.

Neil loved the trip. 'At night we'd go out with Al [Green]'s nephew and he was our passport into the black nightclubs. If we'd been Americans we would've been in trouble. But we told them we were Scottish and we were okay. Some of the guys didn't even know where

Scotland was. They thought it was behind the Iron Curtain and even gave us advice on how to stay in the States.'

Graeme was almost blown away in the trigger-happy town. He chatted to a young lady in a nightclub who thought he was making advances. 'It was my accent,' said Graeme. 'She thought I was trying to pull her so she pulled a gun. Thankfully, it was all smoothed over.'

Back home, the Wets lived off the experience for some time. It had been wonderful, and they loved the tracks Willie had produced. But Phonogram didn't. They hated them, in fact. The record, they said, was unfit for release. Even Willie Mitchell admitted, two months later, 'I've made you sound too black.' The Wets had no choice but to accept the verdict. They went back into the studio, took the master tapes and reworked them, stripping off production layers until they got as close as possible to their original demo sound, which everyone had loved.

'Wishing I Was Lucky' was one of those songs. 'The A&R guy said it was no good,' recalled Tommy. 'We said, "Give us a chance, give us enough rope," and thankfully, he did.'

The Wets more or less produced 'Wishing I Was Lucky' themselves, a song about the blight of unemployment, with overdubs from the original Liverpool recordings. It was released in March 1987, two years after it had been first recorded and almost two years after the band had signed a recording deal.

'The record companies just want you to go and do a big production number,' they moaned, 'then, when it doesn't quite work, they send you back into the studio with another guy and spend another fortune on it.'

The Wets were convinced, more than ever, that *they* knew how they should sound. 'Four heads are better than one dickhead,' was Marti's opinion.

And after a long haul up the charts, 'Wishing' eventually reached number six. 'The fact that song was actually released was a highlight,' said Tommy. 'But we were embarrassed when we saw ourselves on TV. And all of a sudden we had itineraries. And we knew what we were doing the next day and even the next week!'

It was phenomenal. Pop guru Jonathan King predicted the Wets would be 'the biggest band in the world in a year' and even Radio 1's twilight-zone DJ John Peel, the man most likely *not* to like them, conceded, 'They can play!'

Everyone was ecstatic, including Dave Bates. But Elliot, being Elliot, made sure he let Bates know he'd made a big mistake in not giving the boys their own say from the beginning. 'I could have stood Elliot not crowing around the place; then again, he had proved his point,' admitted Bates diplomatically.

The Wets had now become pop stars. And one of the first things Marti did when he received his first gold disc was to present it to May Dorman, his best pal's mum. May still has it on the wall of her Clydebank home.

Marti himself was now being pinned up on a lot of walls. 'Sometimes we get mobbed by screaming girls, but that's because we're a young band,' he said modestly. 'After all, we're not elephant men.'

In the same month, the Wets were to appear on BBC2's *Whistle Test*, alongside, perhaps ironically, The Smiths, but the Manchester band pulled out. 'This was a real turning point for us,' said Elliot. 'The single "Wishing I was Lucky" had been released that same week, and here were five fresh-faced lads from Clydebank playing on the most street-cred TV show on the box – and going down a storm. It was an incredible feeling, knowing that this was the last-ever *Old Grey Whistle Test*. Of course, the boys were more caught up in *Top of the Pops* at this time, but, nevertheless, the *Old Grey Whistle Test* had played host to the likes of James Taylor, Elton, the Doobie Brothers and The Clash over the years, and this was a real status symbol for the band.'

In May the Wets agreed to do a show at the Oxford Ball, certainly the most incongruous place they'd performed in, Shotts prison included. Four young street kids from Clydebank didn't fit in easily amongst the pomp and pretension of the educated élite. It was to be a memorable day for Marti, in more ways than one.

'We'd been hanging about backstage, waiting for the PA to go up, when Marti suddenly announced he wasn't going to play the show,' said a band insider. 'We all thought he was joking, of course. He'd been complaining all day about a sore throat, which, to be honest, we'd all heard before, so we chose to ignore him. Come soundcheck time, he was still refusing to perform, so Graeme then said he'd take over lead vocals, backed by Graeme Duffin. As you'd expect, Marti was livid and took the huff. Meanwhile, we plied him with honey tea and antibiotics. Needless to say, come showtime, Marti miraculously recovered his voice. The fear of being replaced by Graeme worked wonders and the whole matter was instantly forgotten.'

Graeme began the show by teasing a few people when he called out, 'You bunch of Tory bastards!' Marti laughed as he defended his pal's position. 'It was all those birds walking about in frilly chiffon dresses,' he said, 'all crumpled with grass stains on their arses.' A band insider was later to confirm that one of the Wets team had similar grass stains on his knees. Clearly, the boys were having their first taste of attention from professional groupies and enthusiastic amateurs. The Wets made the most of it, took the money and ran.

But that same month they began to pay the price of fame with their first taste of tabloid intrusion. *The Sun* did an old-fashioned stitch-up job on Marti's mum and dad, where John McLachlan was said to be furious his son had changed his name. *The Sun* said, 'He demanded: "What's wrong with McLachlan?",' suggesting Marti had sold the family name down the river. Marti told his parents not to talk to the press again.

At the end of the month, the Wets were off to The Gambia when the East African country was chosen as the location to shoot the video for the next single, 'Sweet Little Mystery'. It was an expensive exercise but also an education. 'There were no roads, just mud and cattle everywhere,' remembered Tommy, 'with thousands of corrugated iron huts where people were living. You drive for about five miles in an area where people have houses and belongings worth fifty pounds then turn a corner to see conglomerates that are worth fifteen million.'

'Sweet Little Mystery' was released in July and even the *NME* loved it. Marti's voice was described in *The Guardian* as 'acrobatic'. Mat Snow, in *Town and Country,* said something more important: the Wets would go the distance. 'Through their unremitting drive and high-cholesterol textures, they have a songwriting strength in depth which suggests their success will diversify and so outlast the fickle favours of their current teeny-bopper audience.' Snow was predicting exactly what the band were hoping for – longevity. But longevity could only come about by being taken seriously, by appealing to more than just teenage girls. The Wets were just beginning a long battle to lose this image.

As the single reached number five, ahead of Boy George and Terence Trent D'Arby, they were asked to support American superstar Lionel Ritchie, a terrific accolade particularly since the band were huge fans of his music. But Marti again developed problems with his voice. And he couldn't sing a note. 'I'll never forget it,' he said. 'We were all in tears. I lost my voice just as the single came out and we were halfway through the tour. It seemed like the end of the world.'

It wasn't, of course. The threat of being sacked and the loss of the Lionel Ritchie gigs saw him head straight for Harley Street. His throat was checked out and given the all-clear. A slight case of psychosomatic illness was diagnosed.

Back in the studio, this time with a producer they rated, the song 'Angel Eyes', which had originally been titled 'Home and Away', was transformed into a sweet soul ballad.

At this time *Record Mirror* interviewed the band, and asked if the Wets were to become another 'style' '80s band like Curiosity Killed the Cat, Swing Out Sister and Johnny Hates Jazz. But *RM* discovered success hadn't gone to their wardrobes. 'Isn't it some relief to find Wet Wet Wet haven't changed at all?' they wrote. 'They still look like a bunch of scruffs pulled out of a football crowd.'

The truth is, although they'd had three successful singles, the lads weren't exactly coining it in. In fact, they'd only just agreed to pay themselves two hundred pounds a week, their first real wage. Elliot warned the band they'd have to sell a million copies of their first LP to pay off the Phonogram debt, accumulated over two years and now standing at £600,000.

Although the Wets weren't earning pop-star wages, they were attracting the attention that goes with the job. Marti told the *NME*, who were still in love with the band at this time, about the problems dealing with being recognised in Glasgow. 'I went out for a few beers with my mates last Friday,' he said. 'We went into this pub and all these lassies started screaming "Therheiz! Itzhim!". And this guy comes up to me and says, "Hey, you're the fucking singer oota Wet Wet Wet. That's ma burd over there – wantae go kiss her?" So I looked over and this fucking woman was a beast, a beast! I says, "I'll sign an autograph, but I'm no' kissin' her." He had big chugs on his face, this guy, and a Local Diehards '75 tattoo on his arm. He says, "Is ma fucking burd no' good enough?" I says, "Well, basically, no. She's uglee!" I thought he was going to ask me outside, but he started laughing and shook my hand and said, "Well, at least we agree on something!"'

Marti's next encounter with a female fan, according to *The News of the World*, wasn't 'uglee'. The singer featured in the first Wets sex-shocker. 'SEX IN THE SHOWER WITH WETS STAR MARTI', screamed the headline, on a story about how Marti had spent the night with a female fan. Allegedly, he and blonde beauty Mandy Lansley had a steamy one-night stand and he 'literally got into Mandy's pants after meeting her' (she lent him a pair of her boxer shorts). Despite losing her boyfriend and nearly getting sacked from her job, Mandy's final comment was, 'I don't regret the night I slept with Marti Pellow.'

It seems the man in question didn't exactly concur. 'I was featured in a scummy tabloid because I had sex with a consenting adult,' he said later. 'I'm human. I copulate. But my first thought was "How are my mum and dad going to take this?". But when I went home they just laughed at me. I got smacked wrists and was told "You're staying in for a week". It did one good thing, though. It stopped the "Marti is gay" rumours for good.' Up until this point no one had actually said Marti was gay in print. The saucy tabloid tale made the Wets, particularly Marti, determined to keep their private lives out of the papers.

Meanwhile, the band's popularity soared as they played more gigs. In August they claimed to have turned down a Madonna support gig to play a football charity match against teams from Frankie Goes to Hollywood and Big Country. A month later, two thousand fans turned up outside a Virgin megastore to see a fifteen-minute promo gig.

In September the band released their first album, *Popped In Souled Out*, which sold over 50,000 copies in its first week of release. It entered the charts at number two and finally made the number-one spot on the strength of the release of the single 'Angel Eyes' in November, which reached number five. *Popped In Souled Out* was to sell 2.3 million copies.

But Elliot, true to form, didn't start spending recklessly. 'On the *Popped In Souled Out* tour he hired a single-decker bus,' recalled Willie Knox. 'Normally, with a big crew, you have a double-decker where everyone can get their heads down. Elliot told us we could "take turns sleeping". The crew told him to go away. He'd cut corners whenever he could. His way was to get people to work on the cheap by promising them gold at the end of the rainbow. But that gold, for a lot of people, always seemed to be too elusive.' Some left the set-up, but then others, such as the highly efficient tour manager Dougie Souness, have stayed to this day.

Although Elliot scrimped as far as the crew went, the band's performances were incredibly successful. And with this success came even more attention from adoring fans. Graeme agreed it was becoming increasingly difficult to deal with it all. 'It's hard enough to keep a relationship going in this game without hassle from groupies,' he said. 'And I'm not interested in girls who are only interested in me because I'm in the Wets.' Graeme must have had a couple of tequilas too many when that quote came out of his mouth.

Nevertheless, there were a whole set of new problems for the band to contend with. The Wets were now all practically joined at the hip. When they were kids they could go home to their mums. Not now. Later that month, they travelled down to Newcastle to film an episode of cult pop show, *The Tube*. Eric McCarthy was the co-driver of the transit van. He had reckoned on a quiet ride with four young pop stars. What he didn't count on was a punch-up in the back of the van. 'We were heading down to a club called The Roxy where filming would take place and blethering away, and then this argument broke out between Marti and Graeme. I think it was about who owned which CDs,' recalled Eric. 'Before I knew it, they were punching lumps out of each other in the back of the van and the other driver and I had to stop, jump in and separate them. It was a temper thing that exploded but no one was hurt, no gumshields were dislodged or anything. In fact, it wasn't so much pistols at dawn as handbags!'

The trip wasn't all disharmony. 'We had been playing a Blue Nile tape for a bit of background music,' said Eric, 'but the boys took it out and stuck in their own tape. They were right into listening to themselves. And Marti told us he'd just had his tonsils out and he wanted to test his voice. So he began singing "Angel Eyes" in the back of the van, unaccompanied. It was amazing. The power of his voice made the hairs stand up on the back of our necks.'

Eric liked the boys. 'Tommy was a real gent and Graeme was nice bloke – he seemed to be the man in charge musically – and Graeme Duffin was also a really nice guy. Neil didn't say much at all and Marti was pretty decent, although a wee bit cocky and without too much to say of real value. But, all in all, they were young guys dealing with this new success. And we could tell that despite the wee battle in the back they really were pals.'

But the Wets landed Eric and his mate in hot water. 'They tried to do us a favour by agreeing to take a taxi from the hotel to the gig and leaving us a bit of free time,' remembered Eric, 'but the tour manager tore a strip off us for letting the boys go off on their own. "You can't listen to those guys," he yelled at me and my mate. And then he said – wait for it, this really made us laugh – "They're just crazy, mixed-up rock stars, man." We had to hold our sides when we heard that one.'

The 'crazy, mixed-up rock stars' (except Neil, of course, who hardly ever put a foot wrong) were actually living up to their billing. Back on the European tour, at an Indian restaurant in Frankfurt, the band had to wait two hours for their orders to arrive. During the wait everyone got drunk and an argument broke out between Tommy and Neil. The drummer and keyboard player ended up wearing each other's dinner. Neil was the one with chicken dopiaz on his face.

But the pair later became friends again and joined in a game of hoop-la, using onion rings as hoops.

The tour was in every sense an eye-opener and an adventure for the Wets. In Stockholm, the boys had to cancel a TV date on Sweden's version of *Top of the Pops* when one of the band missed a flight for the live show. No one owned up to it.

Back home, the intrusion into their personal lives had reached such a level that the boys were even thinking about leaving their parents' homes. 'The time has come to move on,' said Graeme, 'when you start getting your knickers stolen off the washing-line. Especially when my mum has to put up with people peering through the windows to get a glimpse of her son coming out of the bath.'

Neil agreed. 'The neighbours never used to speak to me because I'd been unemployed for two years,' he said. 'Then they saw me on TV and now it's "Hi, Neil, how're you doing?".'

They were also attracting intense media attention – not always positive. Satirical magazine *Private Eye* spied that the Wets had taken more than inspiration from their musical heroes. Van Morrison's lawyers were already taking the boys to task over a wee bit of plagiarism from his song 'Sense of Wonder'. Now, the *Eye* revealed, the Wets had lifted a little bit of Squeeze as well: on 'Angel Eyes' the Wets sang: 'The saddest thing I've ever seen on my TV screen was a dying man who died for his team, the toughest thing I ever heard was that newborn scream in this wicked world.' The magazine pointed out that Squeeze, with 'Heartbreaking World' sang: 'The saddest thing I've ever seen was a football fan dying for his team; the greatest sound I've ever heard was a baby cry in this wicked world.' 'Could they by any chance be related?' asked *Private Eye*. Lawyers for

Squeeze obviously thought so. And the matter was settled out of court with Squeeze and Van Morrison. The Wets said they had 'simply been paying homage to their heroes', and laughed it off.

The legal hassles didn't stop them selling out in their home town for a Christmas concert in front of an incredible ten thousand screaming fans – and clearly enjoying themselves. David Belcher of *The Herald* reviewed the band: 'They have a heart-throb frontperson, the lithe and limber Marti Pellow,' he said, 'who sings and smiles hugely, usually simultaneously.'

Temptations

WHEN Jon Bon Jovi was reportedly seen snogging a young lady in a London nightclub to 'Angel Eyes', the music press saw the incident as casting doubt on Bon Jovi's taste rather than reflecting well on Wet Wet Wet. Journalists in 1988 were taking a more critical look at the band. After all, the Clydebank boys had had three hits; they were well set up for shooting down. In February '88, the Wets were voted by Radio 1 listeners as the Best New British Group at the BPI Awards at the Royal Albert Hall in London. The Pet Shop Boys were voted Best Group. Pat Kane, the singing half of Hue and Cry, hit out at Wet Wet Wet in the *NME*. 'I would rather a girl spend her time with music like The Housemartins or The Style Council or Hue and Cry than with that of people who are exploiting her emotional weakness and instability, like Johnny Hates Jazz, Wet Wet Wet and all the rest of the pin-up groups.' Was this home-grown envy?

Whether they were exploiting the likes of *Jackie* or *Just Seventeen* readers or not, Billy Sloan of *The Daily Record*, the most influential pop writer in Scotland, reckoned the boys were becoming a bit too big for their boots. Of course, he had his own reasons for criticising the Wets – Billy and Elliot had had trouble coming to terms with each other since day one. 'After receiving their Best British Newcomer award at London's Royal Albert Hall, backstage the air turned blue with a torrent of four-letter words and childish verbal abuse,' wrote Billy. 'It seems the Wets were upset because not enough sycophantic inches had been written about their pub-rock sound.' Ouch! Billy Sloan then went on to write that his vote would have gone to The Proclaimers or even The Christians, 'whose musical impact has been much more significant'. Billy seemed to feel the Wets were being burned by the bright lights: 'Maybe all this

PREVIOUS PAGE
Elliot Davis, manager of
Wet Wet Wet, at
Precious HQ

pressure and attention is a case of too much, too soon,' he said. 'Maybe they'll grow up . . . or grow out of it.'

Elliot maintains this was all nonsense, stating Sloany had refused to acknowledge the huge success the band had achieved in their home country. Elliot would argue that it was this aggression – and arrogance – which helped keep them a safe distance from all the phoniness and hype of the business; they were simply being their own men. As success grew, however, the band weren't exactly sure what that entailed any more.

March saw the release of their fourth single, 'Temptation', which was to coincide with their sell-out UK, European and Japanese tours – tours which had Tommy worried as to whether the band could carry them off. They got a nice confidence boost, though, when the single made it to number twelve. Tommy needn't have worried. Wherever the band played, they went down a storm.

But there were accusations that Wet Wet Wet were beginning to believe their own hype. In that month *Q* magazine told of the Amsterdam TV producer who tried to insist a group of teenage girl violinists join the band live on TV. The Wets refused. The Dutch producer said they had become 'like every other tinpot pop star'. As he put it, 'You can shake the hand of Gorbachev but you can't shake the hand of Bono.' The producer's idea was clearly naff, but it was not as if the Wets had been steering clear of the teeny market. The band had nothing against teenage girls. By now they had legions of groupies who followed them round Europe, from city to city, country to country. 'There was one particular set of groupies from Japan who followed the Wets wherever they went,' recalled Willie Knox. 'These girls would always find the band, and this is at a point

when itineraries were kept a very close secret. But their perseverance paid off and they were able to see quite a lot of the boys.' It turned out that the Wets' dislike of Japanese food did not spill over on to their women, and the band members were often to sample the delights of the Orient.

But the tour wasn't all *sake* and sex. One night in Sweden in the Hotel Kom, which was nicknamed Stalag 13, the Wets and crew decided to work out in the gym. Nothing odd about that – except that it was 4 a.m. Everybody was blind drunk. Willie Knox was lifting a 25-kilo weight when Tommy asked to have a go. The problem was the round weights hadn't been secured – and as the bar was being passed over, one weight rolled off the end and landed on Tommy's foot, bursting it open. 'Tommy almost died of fright,' said Willie. 'But we all sobered up quickly and had his toe packed in ice. Marti was pretty gone, because he just looked at us blankly and went off to bed. We grabbed a taxi and took Tommy to hospital but they couldn't do a thing for him except put him on crutches. His foot was so bad the band almost had to cancel a *Top of the Pops* appearance back in London.'

Back home, Tommy's toe healed and life on the road, for the time being, was forgotten. 'You've got to retain a feeling of where you come from,' he said at Precious HQ in Glasgow's Maryhill, where all you can see are grey stone tenements for miles around. 'Anything too flashy turns you off.'

At this point the boys were still hanging out at Aldo's Café in Maryhill. 'I still live with my parents in Clydebank,' revealed Marti at the time, determined to enjoy the best of both worlds. But it was difficult. He told the tale of how he was kidnapped by a taxi-driver

PREVIOUS PAGE
Backstage at Madison Square Gardens on the Elton John tour, 1988

80

who had picked him up in Clydebank, recognised him and, instead of taking him where he asked to go, immediately set off for his own house so his daughters could meet his famous passenger.

Marti, more than any of the others, was coming under a lot of new pressures – pressures to press the flesh of everyone he met and pressures to perform at the flick of a microphone switch. Not that this went against the grain of the man who was a natural show-off, but now he was living his whole life 'on stage'.

Things blew up when the Wets teamed up with Bros and T'Pau for the Brit Music Awards. Gill Pringle in *The Daily Mirror* alleged – falsely – that Marti had head-butted a fan, Jill Howard, wife of T'Pau guitarist Dean Howard and also the band's fan club secretary, after she asked the singer for his signature. Jill was left in tears, and too embarrassed to tell her friends until several hours later.

'Marti didn't do it,' said a source close to the band. 'The Wets have never actually said who did do it, but you can take it from me that it was someone connected to the band, and the singer simply took the rap.' The band later wrote the woman concerned an apology.

'The band were losing it a little at this time,' said Elliot. 'This was the period when the realisation hit them that they were a hugely successful outfit, and there were times when their behaviour was excessive.'

But despite the media criticism, by May the Wets were shoving their column inches down writers' throats when they achieved their first number-one single with the self-produced Beatles classic, 'A Little Help from My Friends'. It cost the Wets two hundred pounds plus VAT and one day in the studio to record the track for the album

Sergeant Pepper Knew My Father, which had been organised by the *NME* for the charity Childline. The song went on to sell 350,000 copies and was at number one for four weeks. The song was originally to have been covered by The Housemartins, but when Hull's finest dropped out the Wets came in and knocked Glasgow's own Eddie Reader off the top of the charts. The single was a double-A side with radical popster Billy Bragg; the teaming was a bit incongruous perhaps, but Bragg said he had no credibility problems appearing on vinyl with Wet Wet Wet: 'It's no time to be squeamish and say "I'm not playing with them",' he said, as if he were talking about attending a Tory conference in a blue suit. 'You have to reach as many people as possible.'

But although the song went to the top of the charts, the band had some misgivings. Elliot later admitted the boys were disappointed that their first number one was a cover, although he believed they had made a good job of layering their own style on to the Beatles hit. But he said the big success, apart from the cash raised for kids, was in being asked to perform on the prestige album. 'We had to force our way on to that album,' said Elliot. 'We badly wanted that credibility but the *NME* hated Wet Wet Wet.'

Roy Carr of the *NME*, who thought up the idea, claimed to be surprised at this interpretation of the story. 'We were delighted to have them,' he said.

The Sun, however, pronounced the song 'drivel'. And warming to its theme, the paper went on to make Marti look a prat for reportedly bidding five grand for David Bowie's guitar at a charity lunch – when Paul McCartney then bid six times as much. 'Poor Marti couldn't compete,' the paper reported. Then the tabloid focused on every difficulty the singer faced, claiming that he was on the wagon and had stopped smoking because of tonsil problems and that, in a bid to ease pressure on his voice, Marti took singing lessons from Helena Shel, who had taught Paul Young and Annie Lennox.

It's hard to say exactly why Wet Wet Wet took it in the neck from the press at this time, although it's probably down to the coverage they were enjoying in the teen magazines. After all, rock writers had been reading blurbs for two years now about how the band were young soul rebels and were deadly serious about their music – and then they were hit by articles in *Jackie*, *Look In*, *Smash Hits* and *No. 1* magazine about the band's favourite food and whether Marti wears a kilt. Wet-watchers could see the boys in glossy pics wearing sponsored Levi's and discover in *Jackie* that 'Marti had always dreamed of getting recognised walking down the street'. 'You just have to get used to all the girls screaming,' was the sort of line quoted.

Marti told the likes of *My Guy* that 'I've got a steady girlfriend who I'm happy with, but it would be better for me to have a tortured relationship so I can sing the blues.'

Graeme, in the teen glossies, claimed he'd been expelled from school for having green hair and then talked of his romantic life: 'I'm not in love,' he said. 'I like to play the field.'

The touring seemed endless, and so did the interviews. They did the usual promotional rounds in Australia but one piece in a magazine there gave more than a hint that the boys had been telling porkies about their ages: ' "I'm twenty-one," said Marti, "but don't call me twenty-one. Better make it nineteen." ' But there was an even more startling revelation when Neil was asked searching questions about little Kylie Minogue, the former *Neighbours* star, who was now having more chart action there than Wet Wet Wet. 'I want to bonk her,' said Neil, uncharacteristically.

As they toured for forty days the band laughed and partied, and punched each other occasionally. But they were always absolutely serious about their music. So serious, in fact, that they were dismissive of Stock, Aitken and Waterman, the most successful record producers in the world at the time. Graeme revealed that the Wets had allowed Stock, Aitken and Waterman, producers of Kylie and Jason, and originators of the dance drum sound, to do a club mix of 'Sweet Little Mystery'. Graeme had chucked the result in the bin. 'It was crap,' he declared, 'and we said "No way!" because we will not prostitute ourselves.'

In the summer tour of Britain the Wets played with absolute conviction and the fans were literally carried away by the performances. At the June concert in Brighton, two hundred members of the audience needed first-aid treatment. But the Nelson Mandela gig with Dire Straits at Wembley brought some negative media reaction. Marti was reported to have yelled at fans 'You're pathetic!' when they didn't chant 'Free Nelson Mandela'. Many of the youngsters didn't know who Nelson Mandela was.

Neither *The Daily Star* nor *The Daily Mirror* were going big on the band. *The Mirror* said Wet Wet Wet failed a popularity contest with Bros on attitude: 'The Wets were bad-tempered, moody and take themselves too seriously, while Bros were helpful and smiling.' Marti was unceremoniously slagged off for not smiling in a photo session with a fan who had won a magazine contest to meet him.

'Marti's not a monkey,' said Phonogram, replying to the accusation. 'He doesn't perform to order.'

Yet, while the fans – mostly young kids it has to be said – loved the concerts, reviewers were labelling them a teeny-bop phenomenon: 'The band are so clean I could eat my dinner off them,' said a Midlands concert reviewer, who didn't take the band, or their fans, seriously. 'You know how it is with babies – one screams and they all start screaming,' she wrote. The reviewer then hit out at Marti: 'Holding notes is no problem for the singer. Finding them is.'

But the fourteen thousand screaming fans in the Birmingham Exhibition Centre in July couldn't have cared less. The Wets even broke the house fainting record. Despite this, the band, claimed Tommy (for the moment calling himself 'Tommi' in the teen mags), had the fame thing in perspective. 'We'll never go off the rails,' he told showbiz writer Stanley Shivas. 'We are making our new headquarters in the old Maryhill Police Station – and London will have to come to us. Everything changes when you hit the heights but, ultimately, you say "Look, this is me, the guy my mammy knows, and my music is what counts".'

Marti agreed. 'We're all getting places of our own now, but we all stay close to our parents. Your ma is the one who knows you best. And you just want to grab a slab of reality. Last week in Edinburgh I was pouring pints behind a bar and some people recognised me, but they didn't think it was me because they didn't expect me to be there. I actually rang the bell and got a staff drink and a share of the tips at the end of the night.'

Despite the dip into 'real life' in the boozer, there were clear signs

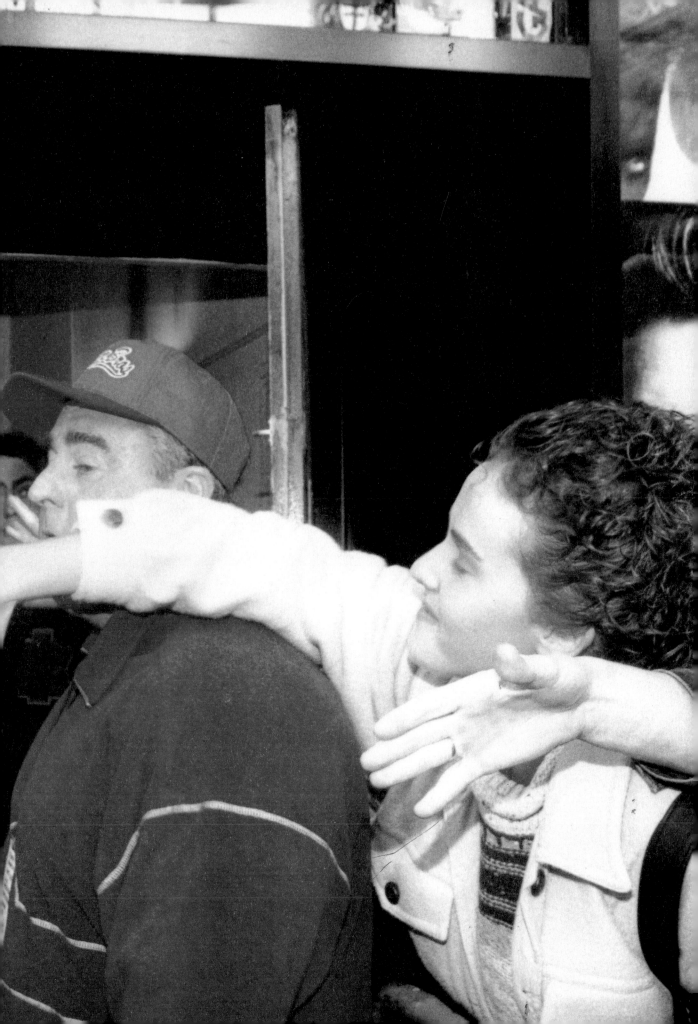

that Marti was successfully developing his showbiz persona. When he met *Mail on Sunday* writer Lesley Ann Jones, Marti planted a telling showbiz kiss on both her cheeks. 'You are mildly irritated by the brazen familiarity,' she wrote, 'the cheek of this callow twitchy starlet with a grin to rival Dover's bleached crags, whom you expected not to like in the first place. At twenty-three, Marti Pellow has yet to grasp the meaning of modesty. So cocky on stage, so self-assured in his delivery, so annoyingly in control of his talent.'

And why should he have been modest about his talent? Not only was there the fan adulation and the media attention, but Marti was actually being asked by another band to sing with them. But he naïvely neglected to tell Phonogram he was doing this 'homer'. The band who poached the Wets' singer were V-V, a female duo. Of course, Phonogram were angry to discover their prize asset was freelancing for a rival record company, Chrysalis.

'A bloke from another record company offered Marti a hundred pounds to sing and he took it without thinking through the consequences,' confirmed Elliot. 'Neither did he consider the effect the move would have on his pals, Tommy, Neil and Graeme who, understandably, were far less than chuffed. But Marti accepted he had made a boob and the matter was forgotten.'

However, Marti was to be tempted many times to do solo projects, but at this point he just wasn't interested in rocking the boat. After all, Wet Wet Wet were now a huge success with five hit singles under their belts. Marti and co had even met Princess Diana and Prince Charles at the Royal Albert Hall for the Prince's Trust Concert. But, more importantly for the Wets, they were now performing with the legendary Joe Cocker and meeting the likes of

PREVIOUS PAGE
Fans reach out to Neil and Marti

Elton John, Mark Knopfler and Phil Collins. The experience set them up well for a mini-tour of the States, going down a bomb in small venues such as the Paradise Theatre in Boston. 'They pack more punch than Wham! and none of their stuff is as annoying,' said the local reviewer.

Twenty-two months previously they had been nobodies. And now it was announced the band were to support Elton John on his American tour. The Wets were delirious. They were big fans of Elton and had even talked of recording his classic 'Burn Down the Mission' from the *Tumbleweed Connection* album.

The Elton gigs, of course, weren't simply handed to the Wets because they were on the same record label. Elliot had been in there pitching hard. 'I was in the Phonogram offices in London when I overheard a conversation with John Reid, who is Elton's manager. He said he was looking for a band to support Elton in America. I waited my time and then cornered him, saying the Wets were the obvious choice. And since we were record company stable-mates, it was good for business. Thankfully, he agreed.'

Not only did the band land a prestigious tour, but Marti in particular won a watch. One of the band recalled how the singer walked off with John Reid's Cartier.

'We were out at dinner one night and Marti was eyeing up John's classic watch. Jokingly, Marti said to John, "Fancy a swap – your watch for mine?" John was stunned that Marti had had the nerve because it was a very expensive timepiece. "Sorry," he replied, "this watch is of great sentimental value to me." But Marti didn't hold back: "Yeah, John," he said, "so is this one, because my mother gave it to me." Astonishingly, John agreed and the two swapped watches. Marti was ecstatic.'

'I couldn't believe the nerve of Marti, and neither could the rest of us,' recalled Elliot. 'But John Reid was clearly taken by his sheer cheek.' What has to be said was that Elliot looked on enviously the whole time.

Marti, in fact, still wears the watch every day, even though he can now afford to buy ten of the same.

Marti said he learned a lot from Elton during the tour, which took them from the Hollywood Bowl to Dallas with five nights at Madison Square Gardens. In fact, Elton was to become something of a mentor. 'He confirmed that family and friends are all-important,' said Marti. 'He was so bored with the yacht and all the Cartier presents and he really lit up when we talked about football. When we played in New York he invited me up to his penthouse. It was amazing, the full works – a massive grand piano and seven toilets. But Elton summed up the silliness of it all when he said: "Look at this lot, eh? I can shit in a different toilet every day." I laughed and said, "No other way, Elton."'

Marti was impressed with Elton John in other ways. The Wets were almost an unknown entity in America, and it was reflected in the treatment they received from tour managers and roadies. It became so bad at one point that the band's dressing-rooms and meals were overlooked. But Marti approached Elton. 'Elton said, "Right, lads, I'll fix it." And he did. He roasted the guy in charge. And then he offered us *his* dressing-room. He's the bee's knees.'

The tour went well, but there were conflicting reports about how the band were perceived by Elton John's management. Some reports, probably coming from the band, said John Reid was so impressed with Wet Wet Wet that he wanted to sign them to his own management company. But others said the Wets had been a pain in the backside and didn't ingratiate themselves with the exalted company. Whatever the truth, 'Wishing I Was Lucky' hit the US charts at number forty-six – before dropping to fifty-two, and then the American dream faded. 'We were one of the five Best New-comers in the *Rolling Stone* poll,' said Marti, 'and then our record company panicked and brought out "Sweet Little Mystery", which was a total pop record, all wrong for America. Radio wouldn't touch it and it flopped. But things got worse. We were on this MCA subsidiary called Uni Records and they closed down the label. You know what MCA stands for? Music Cemetery of America.'

But people in the business reckon that wasn't quite the case. 'The Wets bust their American company,' said one insider. 'The company spent a lot of money on the band and it didn't work out. It's sour grapes. The Wets simply weren't prepared to work their backsides off doing coast-to-coast tours of America – and they paid for it.'

Back in Britain, the magazines quizzed the band about their North American experiences. Writer Caroline Sullivan asked them if they had ever taken drugs. 'I take Resolve sometimes when I have a hangover,' said Marti. 'People have offered me coke but I'm too scared. We smoked in America but it was horrible. I was sick, anyway. And my ma freaks out in case I do drugs because of this business, so I wouldn't do it – because there's nothing to beat the wrath of your ma.'

Graeme also played it safe: 'When you take drugs you don't really know what's going on in your mind. I don't like the sound of that at all. It's disturbing.'

Despite the Pollyanna utterances, the Wets, like many people in pop, did take drugs – nothing serious, but some of the boys do enjoy the delights of hash, particularly when it comes to unwinding after a show.

It had been a demanding year, crammed with hundreds of performances and thousands of interviews. Graeme was tired of the flipside of showbiz. 'It gets to the point where you're sick of living out of a suitcase,' he said. His picture of events may have been discoloured by the fact he had recently split up with his girlfriend.

Marti's romantic life was going better. *Blue Jeans* magazine revealed he was seeing a model called Karen who worked for the mag. In November he revealed he was in love for the first time. 'I know I'm always saying I've never really been in love,' he said, 'but for the first time I think I am. That's all I'm saying.'

On 7 November the *Memphis Sessions* LP was released, the album Phonogram previously claimed was unfit for public consumption. It was a happy moment for the Wets. *The Daily Record* didn't believe the album had been released purely on artistic merit, though: 'Wet Wet Wet must have some affection for these [tracks], their first recorded sessions, for it seems unlikely Phonogram would put out such substandard material. Having said that, it does seem a perfect stop-gap between LPs, what with the record company and all concerned liking a few extra pennies at Xmas.'

Graeme certainly didn't apologise for enjoying the fruits of his labour. 'I'm a socialist,' he said, 'but I wouldn't do this for nothing. I've done that; no way, this is my work and I'm going to eat for the rest of my life.'

In November a huge highlight for the band was appearing at a home-town show in Glasgow's Govan Town Hall before a fanatical audience of nine hundred. The Hollywood Bowl, with its 18,000-seater capacity, was a fading memory.

Chapter Five

Holding Back the Critics

THE New Year saw the Wets sit down and review their success. With five hit singles, a number-one album and a tour with Elton John behind them, they had every right to feel relaxed. But it wasn't enough. They had lost the backing of not only the serious music papers but also of the popular tabloids. The teeny label was stuck on with bubblegum, but the band were determined to remove it.

In January 1989 it was time to begin writing and recording the second album, initially in a remote studio just outside Cornwall, before completing the work at Peter Gabriel's Real World studio complex in Bath. By this time, Graeme was well and truly at ease with the role of production master, controlling studio life. The rest of the band deferred to him – and rightly so. At Real World, the band worked hard and were always perfect professionals. Critics outside the studios, however, were still labelling them bubblegum pop stars. They were right in that the Wets were no longer four working-class boys. They *were* pop stars.

'There was a time the boys would write in Graeme's bedroom,' said Elliot, 'but now it's all got to be done in a recording studio.' The Wets would counter that they needed the studio space to avoid distractions and, if they stayed behind in Glasgow, there would be non-stop interruptions from mates wanting to go drinking or partners looking for attention. Marti, of course, now had to endure – or enjoy, depending on the moment – more demands on his time than the others. He was the one every newspaper writer, radio jock and TV presenter wanted to interview. Fortunately, Tommy helped take some of the weight off. He was fast growing into an articulate spokesman who could not only handle the press attention, but actually enjoyed the challenge of meeting new people and becoming the band's PR man. He put the strains of pop stardom into perspective. 'I don't feel famous,' he said at the time. 'I don't get recognised that often – not like Marti. Sometimes I'm envious of the perks he gets. And sometimes I'm glad I'm not under that pressure. Now we've made it, it would be very easy to say "bye" to the family, sell my house, get rid of the girlfriend, move to London, go to every party, get drunk every night and have a whale of a time. But I'd have a great two years and then I'd end up a mess and the band would break up.'

He chose a 'safer' path back in his old housing scheme. 'I've moved back to Drumchapel and my girlfriend lives with me. She's petrified, has the house alarmed and all of that, and expects it to be broken into at any moment. But I wanted a house that stood on its own, like my parents'.' Tommy also bought a greyhound because he'd always fancied the idea. Not entirely comfortable that it was a working-class thing to do, he called it Biko, after the black South African freedom-fighter.

Marti also felt secure enough to start spending. The money meant he could now give something back to his parents. 'When "Wishing" was in the charts my mum would go down the shops and people would say, "We saw your boy on *Top of the Pops*, you must be a millionaire." And my mum would say, "It's news to me, because he stole ten pounds of the rent money to go down the pub last night!" But now I can fly them down to London for their anniversary. I put them up in a big hotel and gave them a few quid to spend as well. But my mum would go down to the street for an 80p sandwich to take to the room rather than call room-service.'

Marti's mum was still the main stabilising influence in her son's life. 'I put my life in perspective when I go home for ten minutes,' he said. 'One day I could be playing in front of forty thousand people and thinking I own the fucking world and then I fly home, go through the door and there's my mother saying, "Here's a quid, go down and get me a loaf of bread." What are you going to say? "Excuse me, Mother, I don't go and buy loaves of bread without security and an entourage of eighty people"? No, basically, you go and get the bread.'

He spoke about his older brother, John, who was later to hit the headlines for all the wrong reasons. 'I've got one brother,' he said, 'who's now very much living under the shadow of "the younger brother does well". He's two years older than me and has five children. He's unemployed and not too happy, but very proud, and he's really ecstatic for me. I love him so much. I think my family and my community are the only things that keep me sane, from actually believing all this crap around me.'

In March the singer was asked how the new album was progressing, and if there was any pressure on the band to repeat the success of *Popped In Souled Out*. 'Pressure is waiting for your Giro to arrive, not making an album,' he replied.

April saw the Wets perform at an anti-Poll Tax gig at Edinburgh's Usher Hall. They had a lot of friends, they said, who couldn't afford to pay the Poll Tax. At the same time, the band were enjoying to the full the trappings of a pop-star lifestyle, like having the chance to fly to Dubai with a football team. Marti had become friendly with football superstar Kenny Dalglish after he was introduced to him in a restaurant by the then Rangers boss, Graeme Souness. Although Marti was a Rangers fan, as a boy he had seen King Kenny play for

OPPOSITE
Marti's girlfriend, Eileen Catterson

Scotland and had idolised him. Dalglish invited Marti to watch Liverpool play Celtic in the Dubai Cup. Celtic won 4–2 on penalties and Kenny played in the game. Marti had a great time, and a run-out with the players before the match.

The summer was spent preparing for the release of their new album, *Holding Back the River*, and to coincide with this, Elliot was planning Wet Wet Wet's most ambitious project to date. He announced he was organising a free concert to be held in Glasgow Green, where the Wets and other major Scots acts would play in front of an estimated fifty thousand people. The city had never heard of anything like it before. On 11 September 'The Wets in the Park' was launched in the Green and seventy thousand people turned out for the biggest free concert ever staged in Scotland. It was billed as costing £250,000. 'We didn't think anyone would show up,' joked Marti, as the band made ready to showcase the new album. 'But we figured we owed the people of Glasgow something. It was the least we could do to give them a great night out.'

Billy Sloan of *The Daily Record* now sang the praises of the Wets. 'They put their money where their mouth was and gave the kids of Scotland a day they'll never forget.'

Certainly it was, but questions were asked of how the band managed to pull it off financially. *The Sun* asked Marti this – and claimed he 'snarled' at their reporter, saying, 'It's none of your business. Money has nothing to do with it.' *The Sun* also suggested the concert was a marketing boost for the album.

Q magazine had their own theory: 'By the time the final firework goes off, the band will have a concert video in the can and ready for worldwide commercial release and television exploitation. They will also have recorded an "In Concert" performance for network radio broadcast and a documentary for both national and local television. All this coincides with the release of the new single, "Sweet Surrender".'

The Wets dampened down claims they were doing the concert just for their own ends. 'The band are happy to admit that the event combines altruism with self-furtherance but what really distresses them is the suggestion they are lining their pockets instantly,' ran the official statement.

Despite the knockings, the day itself was a delight for the fans. The original plan of the band's tour manager, Dougie Souness, was to have four parachutists drop into the backstage area and then have the Wets in parachute gear run on to the stage, unstrapping packs and pretending to be breathless. But the band refused and Dougie simply called the cops for an escort for the bus. Acting star Emily Lloyd, the girl who showed her knickers in the hit British film *Wish You Were Here*, appeared on the day, and a huge act at the time, Curiosity Killed the Cat, also turned up.

But on the bus to the Green, Marti was clearly stressed and anxious about everything. He complained about Radio 1's Mark Goodier introducing the band, said *Q* magazine: 'How the fuck is Mark Goodier going to introduce us if we've got an intro tape and all? That's gonna look absolutely stupid, right? We don't want to cue off with a fucking Radio 1 DJ. Basically, we don't dig it, man. We don't dig it.'

However, the Wets went down a storm – but so did the weather, dropping 12 degrees. Backstage looked 'like a casualty ward as youngsters were crushed and chilled'. Over thirty were taken to hospital, though none was detained. The show, which also featured Scots act Big Country, had been vitally important, and not just as a launch-pad for the new album; it was a crucial moment in the Wets' survival, Elliot admitted later. 'I think it's fair to say the Wets could have flopped if it hadn't been for the Glasgow Green concert. It gave the boys real credibility and had the serious music press from all over Britain not only sit up and take notice but actually come.'

It wasn't *that* exciting a day, Elliot. Nevertheless, it gave Marti the opportunity to state the new mantra: 'the band has now grown up'. 'The first two singles put us in the pop trap,' he said. 'At that time we were twenty-one and our fans were very much fifteen-year-olds. It's very much a short-lived life in that market. I think we've moved away from that.' Such hope so early.

In September, 'Sweet Surrender' was released. It reached number six in the charts. It wasn't Marti's choice for a first single from *Holding Back the River*: 'The best is yet to come,' he said. Tina Turner, speaking on Radio 1, wasn't thrilled with it either. She described it as ordinary: 'You can tell the guy is a good singer and he's got a good band, but the song is average,' was her verdict.

October saw the release of the album *Holding Back the River*, which eventually made it to number two. In the same month, Tommy and Marti gave their most revealing interviews to date, with Simon Garfield of *20/20* magazine. He spoke to them during their time at a Wiltshire recording studio and asked them about the dilemma of leaving their past behind and growing up in the media eye. Marti admitted it was hard to hold on to old pals. 'Friendships have changed more,' he said. 'For every friend you have, you now have four or five enemies. I walk into a local pub and obviously there's jealousy. You get the loud Scotsman shouting, "Hey you, come here. You! Come here! Kiss my girlfriend!" And suddenly they think you're a kissogram. So you say you don't really want to and he'll go, "Hey, you've changed, man." In fact, they want you to say things so they can hate you. They'll say things like, "Do you want to autograph this for my girlfriend? Personally, I think you're shite." But you've got to bite your lip and sign it, whereas truthfully you want to grab the guy by the neck.'

Tommy said he still saw old friends, but agreed their expectations had changed. 'I have one real friend left and he was in a very similar situation to me – no job and all that. He'd take care of me. When we first got signed we gave ourselves three thousand pounds and I took him away on holiday to Spain and had a great time. But another friend left to work in a bar in Brighton; then, without telling me, called one night to say he'd told the boss I would come down and open up his bar. I hung up. Great friends, eh, when they use you?'

Tommy went further into his past life – and dug a hole for himself in the process. 'The only qualifications I got at school were in art and woodwork,' he admitted. 'All I knew was that I was good with my hands. I was once asked in a job interview if I was honest and I said no. If I could steal I probably would. Even now, when we're on tour, I see a nice lamp in a hotel room and think, "That's a nice lamp," and take it. If I see someone's robbed a bank and no one's been killed, I feel good.'

Tommy wasn't being dramatic in this interview, simply stating that nicking is a way of life in working-class Glasgow, where housing-scheme kids grow up as medium-sized anarchists thinking all property is theft – so why not help yourself? But he learned a hard lesson about being too honest, particularly when the tale went from magazine to tabloid. *The Sun* ran a front-page story with the headline '"I'M A THIEF" SAYS WETS STAR'. Their reporter wrote: 'Superstar Tommy was slammed after confessing he is a compulsive thief who idolises bank robbers.' The story went on to say how Tommy took anything he fancied while on the road with the 'globetrotting supergroup'. And *The Sun* quoted hang-'em and flog-'em rent-a-quote Tory MP Terry Dicks, saying, 'This man needs psychiatric help.' No he didn't. He was just expressing the conflict he felt as a young man from an near-impoverished background who'd become rich and successful in the space of two years.

In Simon Garfield's interview, the two Wets were again making loud noises about wanting to be recognised as serious musicians. Reflecting some months later, Garfield felt the Wets were simply sounding off. His theory was that all pop stars were mad – and the more their wealth and fame grows, the madder they become. 'Wet Wet Wet want to be the exception to the rule that you can't retain your grip on both fame and your old life; you have to abandon one to get the other,' he said. 'Yet, although they said to me that they never again intended to talk about their favourite colour, now their single is climbing the charts they're all over the pop press doing exactly that.'

Consistency did seem to be a problem. If they wanted to be taken seriously, why keep on doing the teeny mags and the glossy photos? 'Most bands did the teeny mags,' said Elliot, stepping on to the back foot.

Christmas-time saw a real attempt at seriousness. The band attacked the charts with a new single, 'Broke Away', an acoustic song that owed more to Celtic music than to soul, and was a far better song than its number-nineteen chart position would suggest. But it couldn't rise above other chart contenders of the time such as Jason Donovan or New Kids on the Block. However, as Elliot would say, 'Where are *they* now?'

Meanwhile, Marti was making greater hits 'in the romantic charts'. *The Sun* reported he had become obsessed with 'Page-Three stunner' Corinne Russell after 'leaving a string of beauties in his wake'. Ex-minder Ray Neilson had sold another story of how 'randy rocker' Marti Pellow was caught in a 'steamy shower romp' and how Marti was constantly pursued by females throwing themselves at him. 'He's a real heartbreaker,' said Ray. He revealed that 'curvy Corinne' turned down further advances from the pop star, however, because she had a boyfriend. The minder said that when the story broke, the pop star 'freaked out at what his mum would think'.

But by the end of the year Marti had eyes for only one woman. He had watched the finals of a Miss Universe competition in Singapore on TV and noticed Eileen Catterson, 'Miss Scotland', who was sent home for being too young. One story suggested he then called the 'raven-haired beauty' at her terraced house in Erskine near Paisley, but her friends said he actually met her at a Rangers club social. Regardless, from the moment they met, the couple were virtually inseparable – though they refused to be photographed together. Marti had had enough of the tabloid intrusion and wouldn't even admit to having a girlfriend. Those close to the singer claimed he was protecting his bachelor-boy status. On Eileen's side, it was argued she was fiercely independent and didn't want to be seen simply as Marti Pellow's girlfriend. But it was agreed that the band could never be taken seriously if they had photographs taken with their girlfriends.

Everyone came to know of the big romance but the couple went to great lengths to play the whole thing down. The Glasgow media backed off and respected their privacy, even – after some heavy persuasion by Elliot – destroying pictures of the couple taken on the street. But Marti's and Eileen's incredible camera shyness was to fade five years later in 1995, when *Hello!* magazine made them an offer, reputed to be around fifteen thousand pounds. So far the couple haven't suffered the *Hello!* curse and are still very much together.

Chapter Six

Wets Run Dry

IT WAS Glasgow's turn to reign as European City of Culture in 1990, a dubious honour where the city reinvented itself for twelve months and put on lots of arty events. The idea was to attract attention from all over the world and to prove that Glasgow had killed off the 'Mean City' image once and for all. Wet Wet Wet, like everyone else, were initially delighted that their city should be spotlighted. In February, the band's European tour to promote *Holding Back the*

Marti enjoys Glasgow's Big Day celebrations, 1990

River kicked off in Amsterdam. 'Marti loves it there,' said a Dutch mag. This was true. There was a period a while back when the singer was actually considering moving permanently to the beautiful Dutch city.

Marti and the others enjoyed the tour, but that didn't mean their home town was forgotten. From what they'd seen, Wet Wet Wet decided City of Culture officials were letting the side down in Europe. Graeme made the headlines in Glasgow's *Evening Times,* slamming the city's publicity machine. 'It was disappointing,' he said. 'We visited virtually every major city, including Berlin, Paris and Amsterdam – but hardly anyone knew about the goings-on in Glasgow. We think the people here are the best in the world, and surely the place deserves more than this non-existant promotional campaign.'

Eddie Friel, in charge of the Glasgow Tourist Board, hit back: 'Who do they think they are, setting themselves up as the spokesmen for the entire population of Europe?'

The Wets argued that they were four guys who had seen more of Europe than you, Eddie. And they had no axe to grind. The band denied they'd suddenly become politicised – even though Marti revealed he didn't pay his Poll Tax: 'Yeah, the bastards have frozen my bank account,' he said. 'But the band has done the political tours – Red Wedge, CND, Greenpeace – now we're going to leave politics to the likes of Peter Gabriel and Sting.'

But it wasn't just about chasing a fast buck. 'Not at all,' said Marti. 'I mean, if we were all that bothered by the glamour life we'd be in London right now. We never did this so we could buy a Ferrari.'

By remarkable coincidence, it was around this time that the Wets threw a glizty party which, alleged *The Sun*, cost a 'whoppin' thirty grand'. The boys hired a floating Glasgow nightclub, the *Tuxedo Princess*, for five hundred friends and family. Marti told the *NME* that his home town meant everything. 'Glasgow has given me a lot; it gave me my hunger, it gave me my passion, my obsession,' he said. 'It's funny, I had an obsession about getting out of the place and now I spend all my time trying to get back in again.'

At least he was now beginning to admit in print that he was a star. 'Listen, I'm a character, all right,' he said. 'People call me a cocky bastard, up there on stage, strutting about like a headless chicken, and I know there's a lot of people want to punch my face in. But on stage I'm arrogant and cocky 'cos I know how good I am. I'm good up there 'cos these songs make me feel good, man, make me feel larger than the lines I deliver. Why do I smile so much?' he said, breaking into a grin. 'I'll tell you. It's fucking hard to be po-faced when you're making this much money!'

The trick for surviving in the business, the Wets were discovering, was to have fun – but not let the world watch you doing it. The band, said Marti, weren't planning to live their lives in the public eye or seek notoriety like The Who or Status Quo. 'We all drink as much as anybody else and we like a good time but the difference is that we do it quietly and no one knows what we're up to. But we're a completely normal bunch of guys that do normal things. No one's ever gonna catch us bangin' some choirboy down a dark alley!'

But it was difficult to avoid the attention. 'Some bloke's bird fancies you because you're on the telly, so he wants to punch your face in. You've got to stand up for yourself, though. I've had to use my fists before today.'

The rest of the band were coping in their own way. 'One day I was walking down the street,' said Tommy, 'and I heard a voice behind me say, "That's Tommy!" I heard it again so I turned round and said hello. They shouted at the top of their voices: "You're a wally!" in front of hundreds of people. But whatever happens to me it must be a hundred times worse for Marti.

'Even having money can be strange. I can remember when I was unemployed I went to buy a settee and the people in the shop looked at me as if I was going to steal it, just because of the way I was dressed. Now when I walk in they recognise me and offer me things for half-price. But we're not rich. We're living on about two hundred pounds a week each. I'm insecure about money. I try to look after it to make sure I'm not cold and starving when I'm fifty.'

Neil also reflected on his own new-found celebrity status. 'Being famous has given me more confidence. I used to be really shy and introverted. But when people come to see you at concerts you become more confident.'

In March the gospel-sounding single, 'Hold Back the River', was released. Marti explained the background to the title track from the album: 'The song is about alcoholism. There was this guy in the Sarry Heid [an infamous Glasgow drinking-den] who was telling me about how he became an alcoholic. Anyway, the old guy raises his glass and says: "You can't hold back this river." And I think, "Nice line, by the way. Thanks very much." You wouldn't have got that in a Covent Garden wine-bar: "There's no holding back the Dom Perignon" doesn't have the same sort of ring to it.'

But in spite of the interesting lyric, 'Hold Back the River' didn't do well, only reaching number thirty-one. Rock writer Stewart

Hennessey talked about the album and explained why the Wets had run dry. 'The white soul boys from Clydebank plunder the blacker scenes of American pop history and float bluesy chords, churchy vocals and sensual soul into the mainstream.' Sounds fine so far. But Hennessey added: 'It's all very well, but while the music might be cleverly crafted, it still blends into blandness, the solid character of the original styles functioning as mere decor for a lot of hollow posturing. In other words, why bother with the Wets when Al Green, Otis Redding, James Brown and a thousand others did it more

Marti in concert, 1990

naturally and better the first time around? Or why compliment an awful band for making a merely boring album?'

What about this attempt to sound like a black soul singer? asked Radio Scotland presenter Peter Easton. Is that not denying your background? Easton asked Marti how he could have learnt the 'soul vocabulary' without actually feeling it.

'Well, as Willie Mitchell says, if you've never been in love, you have to be a good liar, or a good actor,' said Marti. 'When you're growing up, you soak up what's around you. Half my record collection's by black artists. But soul isn't just for guys from Detroit – it's a passion.'

Stewart Hennessey didn't agree, and was then to damn the band with faint praise. 'At the group's SECC gig in Glasgow last week, from tot to granny and everything in between, the fans gushed, blushed, shrieked and screamed at the Pellow person's every gesture.'

This is exactly what the band didn't want to hear. The album was an attempt to get away from the teeny-bop sound of *Popped In Souled Out*. This was to be a mature album, not songs for young screamers. Although *Q* magazine called *Holding Back the River* 'masterful soul-tinged pop', the *Glasgow Herald*'s rock writer, David Belcher, was less generous. '*Herald* Man Gives Wets OK Review', he wrote. 'In the past year, the Wets have assiduously used the "adult" rock press to disavow their teeny-bop following, stressing their musicianly integrity and thus laying claim to serious status, serious sales and greater longevity. On Tuesday night's evidence it seems the plot has failed miserably.'

Alan Jackson of *Scotland on Sunday* summed up the way the media coverage was going: 'Somehow that smooth sound and impressive dentistry began to irritate elements of the press. Reading the average review of a Wet Wet Wet single in *Melody Maker* or the *NME* you would find yourself wondering if the group hadn't inflicted some personal harm upon someone or something close to the writer – head-butted his or her granny perhaps, or wilfully run over their cat.'

Elliot took up the gauntlet. 'I accept that taste is a personal thing,' he said. 'But writers saying they're "talentless" puts you right up a gum-tree, because what they have is a tremendous singer, musicians *par excellence* and songwriting beyond belief. I think it's just a case of having been successful too young.'

Graeme hit back at the bad press and defended the band's attempts to lose their younger following. 'We don't want to end up in the same situation as Bros,' he explained. 'Their second album stiffed, and the danger is that your younger fans grow up and move on to some other group.'

The *Aberdeen Press and Journal* asked Graeme about the clichéd 'second album problems'. 'We had six years to get the first album together, then six months for this,' he offered. 'Under that sort of pressure it was difficult, but we'd say it was better than the first.' The *Press and Journal* courageously waited before putting their reply in print: 'If it was hard for them, how do they think it feels for us having it rammed down our throats?'

Marti then re-chanted the band's mantra: 'Wet Wet Wet are not some Cinderella story. Every day we're winning more and more people over with our songs. Our new record has good lyrics, strong melodies and mature arrangements. It's a big boys' album.'

The big boys were given the chance to prove themselves on 6 May 1990 when they were invited to perform at the John Lennon Tribute

Concert in Liverpool alongside Yoko Ono, Kylie Minogue, Lou Reed, and Daryl Hall and John Oates. The Wets sang 'I Feel Fine'. Another Scottish band, Deacon Blue, did 'Hard Day's Night', and little Kylie, whom Neil had once wanted to bonk, won the fans over with 'Help!'. The concert was a great success.

But meantime Elliot was to upset Radio 1's Gary Davies by pulling the band out of a Radio 1 Roadshow in Norwich to go on holiday. The irate DJ broke the news to listeners and then invited them to write and complain to the Wets, giving out their office address on air. Elliot's reply was that he had insisted the band rest before embarking on a tour. And they needed rest. Wet Wet Wet had been touring constantly in Britain and Europe in a bid to establish an international reputation. In Europe, the fan club was growing, particularly in Holland, Spain and Germany. In Australia, the band really made their mark, but not perhaps in the way they'd imagined. Marti, it turns out, was offered a job as a pub singer way out in the outback. It happened as the band finished their tour and Marti entered a karaoke competition in a local bar. A disguised Marti, with Graeme on guitar, gave a made-up name 'for a laugh' and were gobsmacked when they won. Then the local bar owner offered them a week's work singing in his pub – for beer money. 'It was just a laugh,' said Marti. 'We got on stage and sang a few John Martyn numbers. Next thing we knew we'd won and the guy from the boozer was asking us to work for him. He obviously didn't know who we were.'

Back in Britain, Marti, having adopted a long-haired hippy look, had the band's old enemies, *The Sun*, complaining that he looked 'scruffy'. At home in Glasgow he attended a local nightclub for an after-Pavarotti party. Never the shrinking violet, when he heard one well-heeled lady was willing to donate a hundred pounds to charity if Marti would sing, the pop star leapt up and grabbed the mike. He told an astonished audience: 'I know you've all been to see Pavarotti but I won't hold that against you.' Marti sang his heart out, and the Pavarotti fans went wild.

Another impromptu performance took place a short time later when Marti's girlfriend, Eileen, was invited to a friend's wedding in Paisley. Marti and Eileen rightly turned up late to avoid hogging the bride's limelight but later on in the evening the pop star took the stage with the wedding band and stayed with them right through their repertoire of creaky pop standards. 'Marti does this all the time,' said Radio Clyde DJ Tim Stevens. 'I've seen him at Rangers Football Club socials. One night I was at the same table as him and Eileen, and the band began to play. She turned to me and said, "Watch this, in a minute he'll be up there." Sure enough, up came the cry "Marti Pellow for a song" and he bounded right up on to the stage. You couldn't have dragged him away from the mike.'

In July, Marti returned to his day job as lead singer with Wet Wet Wet when the band were asked not only to perform but also to carry the flag at Glasgow's Special Olympics at Celtic Park. They put on a great show. Marti sang his heart out, and barely paused for breath before sweeping a young lady off her feet for an impromptu dance. The 32,000-strong crowd roared with approval.

The following month, the singer was invited to become Clan Chieftain at the International Highland games, but declined. He was busy buying a new £30,000 BMW – even though he couldn't drive. Eileen was to chauffeur her boyfriend around for some time. 'I've got to learn to drive,' he said, 'and this is a great incentive.'

Marti may have been travelling, but the new single 'Stay With Me Heartache' wasn't. It ground to a halt at number thirty. With 'Hold Back the River' having suffered a similar fate, the Wets took the warning seriously. Neil said later, 'The bad sales definitely gave us a kick up the arse. In fact, we should never have produced the second album ourselves. But you live and learn by your failures just as much as by your successes.'

It was a time when the Wets needed good, credible music press and the *NME* were courted into taking a walk down memory lane with the band as they revisited their old stamping grounds. As reporter and musicians toured Clydebank, we learned some titbits about the young pop stars. Neil revealed that he suffers from asthma and Tommy that he had bought a new Mercedes 190. Graeme admitted he had now fled the family nest and had his own flat above a supermarket.

The first stop on the tour was Clydebank High. 'We didn't want to be there,' said Marti of his old school. 'School offered us nothing. What we did have were dreams of being on *Top of the Pops* and travelling the world. Learning for me meant learning the words of the new Michael Jackson song.'

Tommy agreed he had taken little from the place. 'The school never gave us anything except a sense of humour and how to carry on,' he said. 'It's the town that educated us rather than the school.'

Marti, who was wearing a Rangers shirt, ran with the notion: 'We wanted to use the school orchestra on one of our tracks but the school didn't want to know. It was as if they were saying "When you were at school you didn't show the inclination so why the fuck should we help you now?".'

The band and the *NME* moved on to a mock-tudor-style pub where Tommy used to play the drums when he was fourteen. They talked about the problems of 'staying one of the boys' in an area where most of their friends were struggling to get by. 'If you buy drinks for everybody you're a flash bastard and if you don't you're a tight bastard,' said Marti. 'They'll want to get their turn in even if it's their last couple of quid.'

On they went to the Hub Community Centre, where as seventeen-year-olds the band played their first gig under the name Vortex Motion. 'There were about fifty people there,' said Graeme. 'None of them knew what we were on about. Neither did we. We were shit.'

They took a trip to Arran, an island off the west coast, where Marti's dad used to take him as a boy. 'If you come from a right rough area this is your Costa del Sol,' he explained, revealing that one of his great pleasures in life still was to 'nip down to a seven-quid-a-night pub B&B, get rat-arsed and wake up to a monstrous hangover-cure breakfast'.

The *NME*, on this occasion, loved the boys: 'If there are less affected pop stars out there they're certainly doing a good job hiding it,' they wrote.

But 1990 hadn't been a great year for the Wets. The two singles hadn't threatened the top end of the charts and, although the album sold big, it was very much on the strength of *Popped In Souled Out* and the Wets' live performances. If their Clydebank High teachers had made up a report card for the year it would probably have read 'B-minus. Could do a whole lot better.'

Chapter Seven

The Heartache Stays

IN JANUARY of 1991, Wet Wet Wet didn't look like achieving their ambition of becoming dinosaurs of rock. As a band they had attempted to evolve from a teens' favourite into a serious set of musicians. They had tried to reinvent themselves in the serious music papers, they had grown their hair long and produced a 'big boys' album, a major attempt at black soul, but it had ended up a whiter shade of pale. It was time to write for the next album.

First, though, the band were to take part in another recording project. Ricky Ross of Deacon Blue had pulled together the showcase album of Glasgow songs, *The Tree and the Bird and the Fish and the Bell*, as a tribute to the work of Glasgow photographer Oscar Marzaroli. Wet Wet Wet contributed 'Broke Away'. At the launch of

Graeme Clark, Marti Pellow and Graeme Duffin play in a Glasgow bar, 1990

the album, Marti talked about the Wets' current appeal. Some might have said he was protesting just a little too much: 'Look, we're not U2 or The Happy Mondays,' he said. 'We will never be classed as being particularly trendy as we are popular among people of all ages. But what is wrong with that? When we first set out, our aim was to come up with some classic songs that would appeal to people right across the board, and that is still very much our goal. Elton John, whom we all admire greatly, once said something to us that I always remember. He told us when he had his first hit with "Your Song" he just put his head down, ran as fast as he could and hoped for the best. There was no big plan, just pure adrenaline. That's how the Wets operate. At the end of the day, it's the quality of the music, not all the hype that goes with it, that really counts.'

Tommy agreed. 'Despite all the glamour and the travel, the bottom line is that at some point the four of us have to lock ourselves away in a dingy little room somewhere and get on with the business of writing more songs.'

These songs were changing, and reflecting the changes in the Wets themselves. 'It's the songs that count,' said Tommy.

The new songs written, the band took off to Los Angeles to begin recording for the next album, *High on the Happy Side*, at former Eurythmic Dave Stewart's luxury recording-studio mansion, complete with tennis courts and swimming-pool. By this time, Graeme was completely running the show in the studio while Marti sunned himself by the pool. Graeme organised the backing singers, cajoled the songs into shape, and generally took control of the music. Tommy, meantime, fiddled with his state-of-the-art drum-machine, while Neil tickled his keyboard. Graeme Duffin also began to show his true worth.

After two months of recording, Marti's girlfriend, Eileen, joined them in LA. 'Marti even became the unofficial cook,' said a visiting journalist. 'He was very good. Apparently, his mum had taught him how to make chicken sweetcorn soup, and he really had the knack.'

However, the soup didn't warm Marti and Eileen to the idea of having their photograph taken together. 'As soon as any cameras appeared, Marti shouted "No way!" and they were off,' said the reporter. 'Marti said he'd never been pictured with Eileen and would never allow it.'

The Wets had a fun time in LA. Even Neil showed a side few people catch a glimpse of. 'One night Neil, myself and tour manager Dougie Souness went down Sunset Strip to check out the nightclubs,' said the journalist. 'It was incredible, full of megababes and strange types. We were there a couple of hours and had a few beers and then Dougie noticed Neil had disappeared. He shouted out, "Oh no, he's done it again!" – apparently, Neil has a habit of vanishing. Anyway, we went outside and searched up and down the Strip. Eventually we found him, a bit under the weather, chatting up these six-foot blondes – all five-foot-four of him!'

The impression the reporter gained from watching the band work and play was that they were a good bunch of blokes, although Marti was a little over-sensitive to criticism. But in spite of the many hours spent with the band, the pop writer couldn't get to the heart of the four characters. 'You never really get to know them,' he admitted. 'But what you realise is they are totally serious about their work. If Tommy had spare time he'd fly off to New York to listen to mixes of the songs. That said it all.'

Writers feel that talking to the Wets (with the exception, perhaps, of

Tommy) about the world economy or global warming isn't productive. But ask them about their music and they become totally animated. 'If a song doesn't hold itself together on just a piano or guitar, then there is no song,' said Marti during the LA trip. 'These days, technology means you can polish a shite. That's what happened on our last LP. We went mad with samples and things and used technology to shine a turd. But as soon as you take over-produced songs on the road they fall apart. You can see the fucking holes. This album has been about the basics, about getting the songs right on guitar.'

Graeme agreed. 'This album's our *Sergeant Pepper*,' he said.

'Nah, it's more *Sergeant Bilko*,' laughed Marti.

As well as working on the album tracks and his tan, Marti had to deal with a whole new set of diversions in LA. As movie producers dropped by the Stewart mansion to play tennis, they couldn't fail to see the film potential in the band's handsome frontman. Marti was faced with serious attempts to lure him into the movies, something he was later to take very seriously. But for now he had it all in perspective. 'What was I going to do, tell the rest of the boys I'm off to tread the boards or do a film? They'd do me! They'd kick my fuckin' head in!'

There was no chance the Wets would stay Stateside. 'In England [*sic*] *Popped In Souled Out* went gold. Over here, it went paper,' said Tommy. 'Not so much eighteen with a bullet as ninety-nine with an anchor.'

And they weren't going to 'do a Sheena Easton'. 'Definitely not,' said Tommy. 'She played with us at Glasgow Green and they hate her in Scotland now. They pelted her with eggs.'

Back home, Tommy was about to be pelted with rice when he married his long-term girlfriend, Elaine Gallagher, in Glasgow. The

CHILDLINE
CYCLETHON

press had been warned this was to be a low-key affair. Elaine, understandably, didn't want her big day upstaged by the band. Photographers were held at bay by a collection of beefy bouncers. But plans to downplay the Wets' entry to the Clydeside church were scuppered when Marti showed up in a morning suit, sporting a new beard and rock-star sunglasses – and carrying a silver-topped cane. 'The pic men immediately moved in on Marti, who was looking like the man on top of the wedding-cake. Tommy and Elaine weren't happy at all,' said a watching journalist. Tommy, in fact, turned to Marti and said 'Oi! This is *my* wedding day!'

The couple had a reception in the splendid Airth Castle Hotel near Falkirk. However, the police were called at 5 a.m. on Saturday to investigate claims that a room was being damaged and furniture hurled about the hallway. In traditional rock-star fashion, Graeme was charged with committing a breach of the peace and thrown in the cells.

Back in the world of album promotion, the Wets took to playing special acoustic sets for the press to introduce the new, more adult-sounding songs – again. The band's earlier influences of Otis Redding and Al Green were now replaced by the more mellow sounds of The Eagles, James Taylor and Little Feat. At a set in London, the *NME* compared the Wets wonderfully to the Everley Brothers or The Lovin Spoonful at their sweetest. Things looked good. The Wets were now playing in down-to-earth clubs like the 'less-than-palatial' Calton Studios in Edinburgh.

Trevor Pake in *The Herald* wrote of the new gameplan. 'The first time round they gained an image as vacuous, grinning, teeny idols,' he said. 'This time, they want to follow in George Michael's footsteps.' Fine. But in the background there were problems. 'There is the rumour

OPPOSITE
The Wets get on their bike for charity

FOLLOWING PAGE
Marti takes a moment . . . in concert, 1992

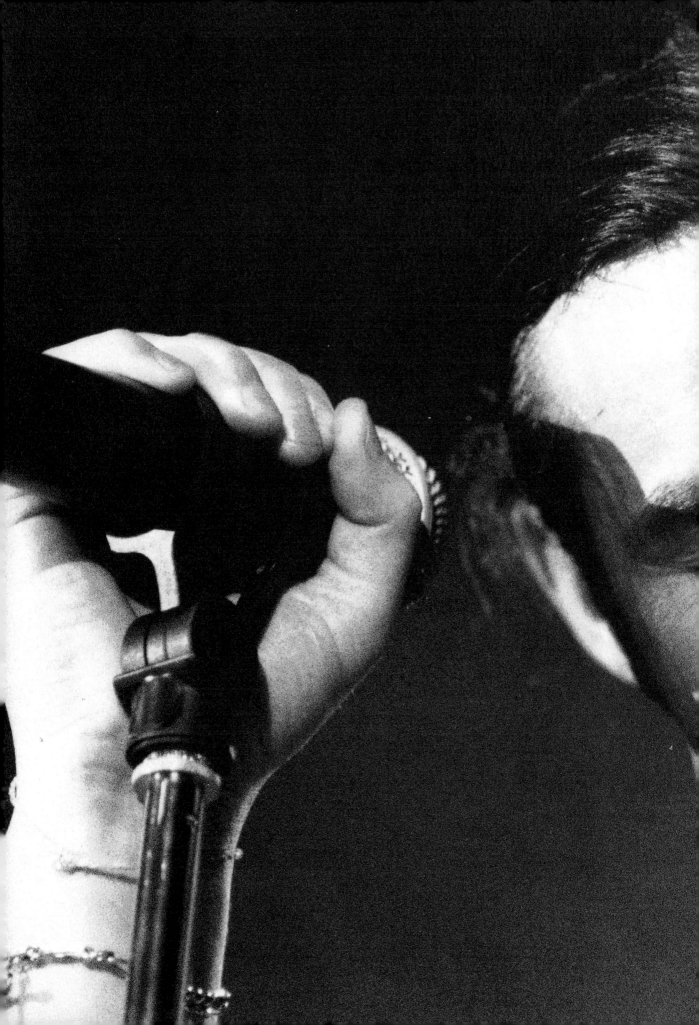

the album is postponed for fear it won't sell,' wrote Pake. 'And the problem with the attempt to appeal to grown-ups was that grown-ups failed to appear.'

Alastair McKay of *Scotland on Sunday* was equally doubtful about the change of direction. 'Something has happened to Marti Pellow. In more innocent times, when Wet Wet Wet were popular, his boyish face came etched with a Charlie Chester grin. It was a smile with a life of its own, big enough to touch hearts at the back of the large theatres, bright enough to light up the bedrooms of a thousand teenage girls. Then Marti and his group did something foolish. They went away and tried to make a record which would earn them an adult audience. They came back from Los Angeles with a spruced-up sound and ideas about the meaning of soul, launched themselves into an exciting new phase of their career – and quite spectacularly and incontrovertibly flopped, belly-up, in the mire. They sound like a pub band playing soul. The band can play. But it's correspondence-course soul, where the songs yield no secrets, only well-learned mannerisms. Their music dances with its handbag on the floor.'

Ouch! But it gets worse. 'Does your heart go out to the man with the Californian tan? Suddenly and emphatically, the answer is *no*.'

It seems the Wets could do no right. They had been chastised for being teeny, and now they were being slated for attempting to produce something more serious. The first single from the new album, 'Make it Tonight', released in September, didn't cause too many ripples in the rock pool. But Marti was philosophical. 'Success in the charts is always great,' he said, 'But we've been out of the limelight for a while so I wasn't expecting too much.'

Just as well. The song only reached number thirty-seven in the

OPPOSITE
Reaching for the high notes, 1992

charts. 'We made a mistake leading off with it,' Elliot later admitted. But the next offering also proved to be a turkey. 'Put the Light On', released in October, only made it to number fifty-six. The press had their knives out: *Scotland on Sunday* headlined with 'Chart success runs dry dry dry as Wet Wet Wet flop'. William Murray wrote: 'After four years of fairytale fame, fortune and adulation from teenage millions, they got serious; they made the old mistake of wanting to be respected, not adored. It hasn't worked.' The Wets, he claimed, could be following their 1970s predecessors, The Bay City Rollers, into oblivion. 'In trying to rid themselves of teeny-bopper taint,' he said, 'they appear to have been bitten by the hand that fed them and lost their audience.'

Marti spoke of the dichotomy to Radio Scotland's Peter Easton. 'Right at the beginning, for about three weeks, we were seen as a credible band, but then *Popped In Souled Out* was a teeny-bop phenomenon. If you were in a pub you couldn't say "I like Wet Wet Wet" because your wee sister liked it or your ma.'

Neil agreed that *Holding Back the River* hadn't been the answer to winning over the critics. 'We thought we were the bee's knees,' he admitted. 'We got self-indulgent.'

But Tommy was to recite the band's second mantra: melodies were all-important. 'The one road we've stayed on is quality melodies – the songwriting craft rather than the production craft.' The difficult part was selling that to the media, and by the media that *didn't* mean *Smash Hits* and *No. 1* magazine.

Marti maintained to *Melody Maker* they'd stayed on the right road by not selling themselves down the river. Despite the mixed metaphors, his point was a serious one. 'Get seen with the right people, break bread with the upper crust, take yourselves away from things you relate to? That's not us. You're sold like a tin of beans, but you've got to be your own tin of beans.'

But the serious music papers reckoned the Wets had to carry the can for their own publicity strategy. *Melody Maker*, slightly tongue-in-cheek, suggested the problem was Marti's smile: 'Always so depressingly happy, smug, incorrigibly pleased with himself, nothing about him ever suggests he's struggled for his art. No one, save a few million women, could love a smile like that. You hate him, you fucking hate him. How does it feel to be the most hated man in pop?'

'I don't give a fuck what people think about me,' Marti replied cheerfully. 'I really don't give a fuck.' And he wasn't about to 'sell out the band and buy in to a solo career', he told Radio 1's Simon Mayo. 'It'd mean I'd be an end in myself,' he said. 'And the good thing about being in a band is coming down in the morning and seeing your mates.'

Despite their insistence that they'd left politics to the likes of Sting, the Wets were still sounding off about what they saw as injustices. In *The Daily Mirror* the band slagged off the YTS scheme. Marti said it had been a total rip-off. 'We were forced to join the YTS scheme when we were sixteen but quit after three months,' he said. 'Kids on YTS get insulting wages and rarely receive training.'

Elliot chipped in to restate his claim that the Wets still had their feet on the ground. 'What I'd like to see respected is the fact we've kept the Wets' business here in Scotland. They live here, they work here, they bank here, other businesses thrive here as a result of them – but it's totally ignored. Take Jim Kerr or Edwyn Collins, it's *whoosh* – straight off down to London at the first hint of success.'

Continued success was eluding the band, however. Release of the album *High on the Happy Side* was delayed until January. Things looked bleak. Graeme began to recognise a hellish possibility. 'We're not going to have any hits here,' he muttered during an interview. 'This album's our most accomplished yet, it's a year of work and it'll sell ten thousand copies. It's going to disappear on us. I can't handle this.'

But there was someone out there looking after the Wets. One song was to rescue their disastrous twelve months and justify the two years spent in the studio. Former Radio 1 DJ Jakki Brambles, now living in San Francisco, had interviewed the band in LA. She was given a sneak preview of the album. 'I told Elliot that there was one song on the album,' said Jakki, who has a better ear for a hit record than most, and who, years before, had played their demo on her show on Ayr's local radio station, WestSound. 'I told him the song "Goodnight Girl" was a number one.'

Graeme Clark didn't agree, however. 'It's just a silly wee song that was written in five minutes. It'll never do a thing.'

Chapter Eight

Goodnight Girl's Kiss of Life

JAKKI BRAMBLES, thankfully for Wet Wet Wet, was proved correct. At the start of the year, the band's strategy of playing club-sized dates to regenerate a buzz worked. 'It had to,' said Elliot. 'This was the last-chance saloon for us.' The single 'Goodnight Girl', wrongly said to have been written by Marti for Eileen Catterson – in fact, it was written by Graeme and Neil – was released on 23 December and shot up to number three. One week later Radio 1 DJ Bruno Brookes was heard to cry: 'Britain has a new number one. The boys from Glasgow have done it.' The song stayed at the top of the chart for four weeks, and record company bosses, quite understandably after two previous duds, opened the champagne bottles.

Nick Rowe, marketing director of Phonogram, explained how important the single was. 'It takes a lot of time and expense on an artist to reach the sort of older people who don't habitually go into record shops,' he said, 'and we were beginning to conclude that we could sell Wet Wet Wet albums without hits, although obviously not in the same quantity. But with this single we got them on *The Des O'Connor Show* and other mass-market programmes. And it's a good old-fashioned pop song.' He could now see the Wets as having cross-over appeal, and as such targeted the grown-ups.

But although 'Goodnight Girl' had a more 'adult' sound, it wasn't the record the Wets would have chosen to be number one. While it was their first self-penned chart-topper, they felt it lacked strong musical credibility. Nevertheless, Elliot Davis was delighted at the success, if only because it forced a huge slice of humble-pie down the throats of the critics. He blitzed off a letter to a national newspaper which had written them off, saying: 'Reports of our death have been greatly exaggerated.' On the strength of the single, the new album *High on the*

PREVIOUS PAGE
At the People's Palace in
Glasgow, 1991

Happy Side, launched on 27 January 1992, shot up the charts, knocking Simply Red off the number-one position.

Coincidentally, Elliot took the opportunity to trumpet in *Q* magazine that 'Marti Pellow has more talent in his penis than Mick Hucknall has in his entire body'. Tim Kellett of Simply Red responded: 'He said that? Well, it's a bit childish, isn't it, but then Marti Pellow has thin lips. And you should never trust a man with thin lips.' Poor Marti. He hadn't even said a word. But at least he and Elliot could afford to gloat. And what's wrong with a little music biz slagging? It sells magazines. *High on the Happy Side* had at least shown the strength of the Wets' fan base, who were eager, if not entirely discerning.

Graeme said the fall and rise of the band was all too much to take in, but Marti was more self-assured. 'Anything we've achieved has been through hard work and the belief the Wets are a great band. That's something you need to have in order to get through when things are not going so well.'

But, once again, the band fell foul of the Serious Music Press. The *NME* hated the album. 'It's one of the worst pieces of over-slick, pompously presented, self-congratulatory nonsense I have ever heard,' said their reviewer, who went on to add: 'Why do even tramps under Waterloo Bridge hate Wet Wet Wet? Because of Marti Pellow's bastard grin.'

Melody Maker's Jim Arundel went that bit further in his antipathy. 'Wet Wet Wet are the palest, limpest, most talent-free cock-brains in pop. "Goodbye [*sic*] Girl" is worse than drivel. It's smug, self-conscious and meaningless drivel. Fuck off to Butlins until you have something real and true and honest to say and have the wit and voice to convey it.'

But Q magazine were more positive (just). 'The result is their best album yet, a pop record which is mature and complicated as well as being fun and whistleable. *High on the Happy Side* is a return to basics, although basics for the Wets are over-layered harmonies, complex arrangements and lyrics which make no sense in any European tongue.'

Craig McLean, in *Scotland on Sunday*, believed it was their best album yet. 'But the albatross of teen stardom weighs increasingly heavy,' he added ominously.

By late January, the band were sounding confident and talking about taking on America, not at all shaken by the news that fellow Scots popsters Hue and Cry and Big Country had been dropped by their record labels. Marti did agree, however, that the previous year had taken its toll. 'It was the most difficult period we've been through. But now we've no qualms about getting in a tour bus and doing a hard slog round the major cities for a year.'

Yes, the idea sounded fine, Marti. But those close to the band said that this would be unlikely to happen. 'Marti may have liked the *idea* of touring in a bus, but perhaps not the reality,' said a band insider.

However, the bad year had left a positive legacy. 'In a funny way,' said Nick Rowe in *The Sunday Times*, 'I think the failure of the recent singles and the hard times have reinforced their down-to-earth approach. They've kept their feet on the ground, stayed close to their roots in Glasgow, and they've grown up.'

Tommy's thoughts echoed that feeling. 'I've learned a lot in the past few months. When we had our first hit everyone told us we would be stars. We thought the world owed us a living, but the first time we tried to break America we came right down to earth. Not long ago, these same people wanted to write us off. Now we've learned not to listen to other people or worry about what they're saying.'

It was time to showcase the album with the 'Lip Service' tour, and in March the fourth single, 'More Than Love', was released. It just made it into the Top Twenty at number nineteen. The band appeared to good reviews and Marti's vocals were now said to be greatly improved. Their mature-sounding set included songs by The Average White Band and The Temptations. Cliff Richard – or 'Cluff Richurd' as *The Daily Telegraph* rock critic thought he'd heard, having a dig at Marti's accent – joined the band on stage at Wembley. Cliff later talked about recording a version of 'Goodnight Girl' for charity and said he wanted the Wets to write for him. The band thought it nice to have the recognition – but they'd rather it had come from Elton John or The Eagles.

Elliot was guarded in his thanks to 'Cluff'. 'It's nice that Cliff rates the band so highly,' he said. 'But I wouldn't say he was one of the influences in their musical career.'

Neil wasn't at all excited about writing for Cliff. 'We're not The Beatles, where we can turn out hits for everyone. If we write a good song we want to record it ourselves.'

The Daily Telegraph's rock man, David Cheal, didn't like the London show. It lacked subtlety and style, a bit like Marti, he said, who wore threadbare jeans, scuffed shoes, a sleeveless shirt and a greasy ponytail. Alan Jackson of *The Times* caught the Birmingham gigs and said the band's eleventh-hour reprieve from what seemed to be their fate pre-'Goodnight Girl' must have been 'a mixed blessing'. And *The Daily Mail*'s music critic didn't like it either: 'There was altogether too much homage to heroes, too much contrivance, and too little of the essence of the soul music they purport to update and reinterpret,' said a review.

The band were used to all this by now, but that didn't make it any easier to swallow. They were still impressing the *Smash Hits* reviewers but not the adult press in the way they so badly wanted to. Sure, they were glad the concerts had sold out and that they had such a strong core of loyal fans. But they had the feeling they were preaching to the converted and were worried they weren't winning the battle for the more mature fan, the kind who bought tickets to see Simply Red and George Michael.

In June, the 'Lip Service' EP came out and hit number fifteen. The summer shows that followed were brilliant or predictable, depending on which review you read. The Wets played the G-Mex in Manchester to twenty thousand fans over two nights, and Marti was wearing his riverboat gambler outfit. The Manchester *Evening News* felt the Wets had proved they had staying-power. 'Unusually, the fourteen-year-olds who fell in love with [Marti] in 1987 did not cast him out like an unwanted Sindy doll. They're still screaming at the age of nineteen.'

The *NME* were at the Sheffield Arena concert in July: 'Pellow is a man passionately, hopelessly and unashamedly in love – with himself.'

Whatever the mixed thoughts of the band, they continued to make news with their ground-breaking promotional ideas – or at least Elliot was. It was announced the band were to play a free concert from the Scottish island of Arran on 13 July, which would be broadcast live on Radio 1, with ten thousand people expected there.

Radio 1 had never before interrupted their daytime schedule for a live concert, so it would be a first for the station, for the Wets – and for Arran. But the organiser behind the Radio 1 roadshow, Jim Sherry, said that problems with Elliot almost had the gig cancelled – and seriously threatened the Wets' reputation with Radio 1.

'Problems developed when Elliot announced the Wets would also be doing an open-air gig at Edinburgh Castle in September,' said Jim Sherry. 'We had billed the Arran gig as the only outdoor event and we could now see tickets for the show fall through the floor – Edinburgh is a whole lot easier to get to than Arran. Elliot tried to justify adding another glamour outdoor event by claiming it wasn't part of the Lip Service Tour and, strictly speaking, he hadn't broken any promises. It was a pathetic excuse. When I heard he'd been advertising the Edinburgh Castle show I called up and gave him dogs abuse. It'd been five months of work to set this up and he was likely to blow it out of the water. And Radio 1 had really gone out of their way to trail the Wets.'

'This is all bollocks,' said Elliot. 'This guy has never been involved in the music business and he had no say in the organisation of the Wets. The band's performance had been jeopardised so often, I had to take control. And thanks to Dougie Souness, the concert went ahead.'

Elliot, says Jim Sherry, had threatened to pull the plug on the event. 'He said he'd pull the boys out and that, to me, was the absolute end. My reputation and the entire plan would have been dead so I called one of the top bosses at Radio 1 and told them of Elliot's threats, and said that Elliot was doing this because I'd told him what a worthless wee man he was. A few days later, I heard that

BANK OF SCOTLAND
6 PICARDY PLACE, EDINBURGH
80-02-34

15th March 1988

Pay Shelter Rebuild Project   or Order
Eight thousand pounds   £ 8,000

I.Y.S.H.

I.Y.S.H.

'You can't close your
eyes to what's
happening out there'

Elliot was given a not-so-gentle ultimatum: get his boys to Arran or the band's name would be mud at Radio 1. The station, remember, was still upset at the band for pulling out of a Gary Davies roadshow that year. The result was that Elliot backed down and sent a grovelling letter of apology to Radio 1. I managed to get a copy of this, which I still have.'

Jim Sherry had previously met Wet Wet Wet when they were recording *High on the Happy Side* in Los Angeles. 'I thought the boys in the band were really great,' he said, 'and still really excited about their music. They'd be calling us over to listen to new tracks all the time and play for people around. Although I'd never listened to their albums, I was really dumbstruck when I heard Marti sing one day at the piano. But when I met him in Arran he gave me a snub. He didn't want to know. I had to ask him if he'd do an autograph for one of the first-aid nurses, who had given her time for nothing, and he said, "I'll see if I've got time." He didn't do it. Tommy, however, was completely different. He came over to me and said, "Thanks for all the effort you've put in, Jim," but I was so sickened by all that had gone on with Elliot, I just didn't want to know. What should have been one of the best days of my life turned out to be one of the worst. On the boat going over I wanted to drown Elliot. The thing about him is that he doesn't know when to stop pushing. And when he goes too far it backfires on the band.'

The Wets themselves had a testing relationship with their manager. And it continues. But the band, says Elliot, have the final say. 'At the end of the day, if they don't want to do something, they don't do it,' insists their manager. 'I can only advise them. But they know I'm usually right.' He admits that, as the manager, he has to keep his distance. 'Oh God, we're not pals, if that's what you mean. I always say to them "I'm not your mother, I'm the guy who has to say no!". It doesn't happen very often though, and you like to think there is no hidden agenda. There was a time when they all ganged up on me and it was over the release of a track from the last album called "Blue for You". I said, "You're mad. You must release it." I was right. The record they wanted was a flop and my choice would have been a smash.'

Tommy explained the band's thoughts on their mercurial manager. 'We know he gives people a tough time, but this is a tough business. And at least we know he's fighting our corner.'

Regardless of the hassles with Radio 1, the Arran concert went ahead. And despite predictions of heavy rain, the sun shone for the ten thousand faithful boat people. It was a big success. Ayrshire

Health Board gave out free condoms on the day and Marti wowed the fans with his tartan gambler gear.

The Edinburgh Castle gig went down just as well. The Wets played Scotland's top tourist attraction on 5 September with the lighting, as Neil poetically put it, 'provided almost magically by the twinkling stars'. The Wets played a great deal of *High on the Happy Side*, the show was a huge hit and the band could claim to have made a little bit of history. But fans, who included Paul Newman's daughter, Jennifer, who had flown in specially from Los Angeles, didn't know Neil was playing through a great deal of pain. At a pre-concert football match he'd been flattened by Marti – and ended up with a fractured nose. To add to their problems, during the show Graeme was singed by a flame thrown during the fireworks display.

The hit concert run continued into October when the Wets realised a lifetime ambition by playing the Royal Albert Hall with the forty-piece symphony Wren Orchestra – proceeds going to the Nordoff Robbins Music Therapy charity. Graeme was struck by the magic of the moment: 'It all felt so natural and right,' he said. 'I had to keep turning round to make sure the orchestra were still there.' This particular charity captured the hearts of the band and in the following years they were to put more time and money into providing disabled kids with the chance to make music.

Tommy explained why they became involved. 'The Wets don't go into pubs and open bottles for charity,' he said. 'But, nonetheless, we try and do our bit. I suppose it's because of guilt. You see so many people who are desperate and you just can't stand back totally. We grew up in an area where so many people are struggling. You don't forget any of that. And when you find yourself financially comfortable in a successful pop band, you can feel bad. You just can't close your eyes to what is happening out there.'

The year wasn't all big crowds and symphony orchestras. In November, Marti was at the People's Palace in Glasgow kissing fifty-eight-year-old loo-lady Agnes Quinn, after she had won a prize for the top loo. But that same month he was almost kissing goodbye to Planet Earth when he was nearly electrocuted after technicians crossed wires during a recording session. Still, it had been a good year. *High on the Happy Side*, thanks to 'Goodnight Girl', had gone platinum.

Chapter Nine

Champagne and Shampoo

IN THE New Year of 1993 the band were working in the studio writing songs for the next album. Elliot, meantime, was arguing – no change there – with the organisers of the annual Brits Awards, when Wet Wet Wet failed to be nominated. 'I wonder what on earth you have to do to get a nomination,' he said, claiming there was a hidden agenda.

In April the band released a live version of 'Blue for You' – the song Elliot had predicted great things for – with the profits going to Nordoff Robbins Music Therapy. The single made it to number thirty-eight. Meantime, Marti's loyalty to the band was being severely tested as the acting offers came thick and fast. But, strangely, it was Tommy, now father to baby Taylor-Elaine, who realised his own secret acting ambition. Without a word to anyone, the pop star had signed himself up with an acting agency, and landed a role in a Scottish TV soap, *Take the High Road*. 'I was an extra for one episode,' said Tommy to *The Evening Times*, 'and no one knew who I was. I didn't tell any of the band about it because I couldn't really explain why I was doing it. I suppose it's because I've done so many different things with the band, that it really left me with the feeling anything is possible. Anyway, it came about while I was watching TV one day and I thought I'd have a go. I went down to a theatrical agency and signed up. They didn't have a clue who I was.'

Tommy laughed as he recalled the band seeing him in the programme. 'There was a lot of delight in seeing the shock on their faces as I became Man Drinking At Bar In Glendarroch.' Tommy was paid fifty pounds for his performance but wasn't impressed. 'It was one of the worst experiences of my life,' he said later. 'They treat you like dirt. You don't get to change or have make-up put on. You look

PREVIOUS PAGE
The band show off the new Clydebank strips as part of the sponsorship deal

grotty – and the stars look great. I won't do that again. Not until Hollywood calls me!'

The acting episode wasn't about a man in search of a spotlight – after all, Tommy had played drums professionally since he was a teenager. He was just looking to test himself in other areas. Already, through his experience with the Wets, he had become the band's best communicator. 'I'm the salesman of the band, all windswept and interesting,' he joked, showing a nice line in self-deprecation. 'I suppose when we go on chat shows it's me or Marti who does the talking. And we can only do that because we've changed with being in the band.'

Tommy, at this time, maintained that he and Neil were the band members least likely to be swept away by stardom. 'I'm a pessimist,' he said, grinning. 'I take the view it could all end tomorrow. That's why I'm the one in the band who thinks about the pension policies. And with a wife and baby daughter you have to be even more focused.'

Tommy's family were now his absolute priority. 'We have a family rule,' he said. 'There is a maximum of three weeks we will spend away from each other.'

While his family offered Tommy some form of structure, Marti's life was still a balancing act between being a pop star and an ordinary Glasgow guy. 'He would stay at my flat when he came round with Eileen,' said long-time friend and model, Susan McKechnie. 'At the end of the night he'd think nothing of crawling into a sleeping-bag on the floor. There's nothing pop-starry about him. He'd rather have tea at his mum's than in some swish restaurant.'

'A few weeks ago I was driving through the Partick district of Glasgow,' said DJ Tim Stevens, 'when I noticed a huge crowd of kids gathered round a chip shop. It seems that Marti had been passing, saw all the kids hanging around and stopped to buy the lot of them chips. When he saw me, he just shrugged his shoulders and smiled.'

But in trying to lead a normal life, Marti is more exposed to the attention of strangers than other stars who get lost up their own entourage. 'No one would deny that the band and Marti are affected by the success,' said Elliot. 'But not as affected as they could have become.'

In March, Marti achieved a very different type of recognition when he actually appeared in *The Broons*, a traditional newspaper strip cartoon featured in *The Sunday Post*. The paper broke with tradition and featured the Glasgow pop star. Marti's family were tickled pink. Jings Crivens, Marti! Whatever next?

The success of 'Goodnight Girl', which clearly had rescued the band in their darkest hour, wasn't going to sustain them much longer. Their new songs had to be even better or it wouldn't be long before the critics started sharpening their pencils to a point that could draw blood.

That same month, on 23 March, Marti's birthday, the singer talked at length to *The Evening Times* and repeated the Wets' mantra: we must write good songs and will then be taken seriously. The extensive talks took place at the new offices of the Precious Organisation in the north side of Glasgow, set at the side of a canal scraped to allow boats access to the whisky bonds and warehouses. The superstar and the ordinary Glasgow bloke appeared at one sitting. Marti walked into the room wearing the bright green jacket he had worn on *The Michael Ball Show* the week before. 'Do you like it?' he asked, accepting the compliment that this was a great-looking jacket. 'Comme des Garçons. It cost me fifteen hundred quid. And look at it. I went out for a curry last night with the girlfriend and spilled my dinner right down the front. What a nightmare, eh?' He wore the curry stain like a badge. It was a nice sign that he didn't take himself *that* seriously. But he admitted that other people weren't really sure what to make of him. 'They often have a preconceived idea of you from TV or the papers and then when they meet you they say, "You know, you're normal!" But I say, "I hope ah'm fucking not!" But it's still difficult to know what people expect of you. So what you do is just be nice and it cheeses off the ones who'd like to have a go at you.'

He grabbed a mug of tea and Kit Kat and thought hard about the consequences of living in the city he loves. 'In Glasgow people either want to shake your hand or punch you in the face,' he said, muttering the now-famous quote. 'That's why, if I walk out of here today and someone asks for an autograph, I sign it. If I don't they'll think I'm a pain. But it's only five minutes of your time and it's more hassle to refuse. But at least you know where you stand here. And that's what you've got to respect about Glaswegians. I couldn't live in London. Here, there is a sense of community. I love this city. It's honest.'

And there are friends and family. The pop star was by now living in a fabulous house in the picturesque town of Helensburgh but friends said he still spent much of his time at his parents' tiny bungalow in Clydebank. At that moment Tommy walked in with a birthday card. Marti opened it. 'Two quid,' he said, laughing,

holding it up. 'I'll get myself a drink. Thanks, lads.' It was a complete contrast to the conversation we had been having about a silver Ferrari he was planning to buy himself for his birthday. So what was it all about now, Marti? Was Mark McLachlan gone for ever? Critics would say it's easy to play at being down-to-earth when you're up with the stars. 'My mates are boys who have known me for years when I used to piss my pants at school,' he said, shaking off the accusation. 'When I go up on stage they say, "I can't believe you're up there, it does my head in watching you." But I know when I go up on stage it's like putting on a coat. I've got enough savvy. Yet it's all so weird. I can fly in from somewhere by helicopter, ride a stretch limo, meet up with an old mate and hear myself say "By the way, has your Giro arrived?". It's perverse, but it's also funny.'

Marti wasn't trying to say he hadn't been affected by fame; after all, he'd sung with his mate Joe Cocker and Otis Clay, met Eric Clapton (who asked Marti for *his* autograph), and of course, Elton John. 'Seven years ago I wouldn't have been able to speak to you like this,' he said. 'I would have felt intimidated. But success brings confidence. Yet, you don't forget things. People will sometimes say "What's a thousand pounds to you?", but I know people go out in the pissing rain and snow for a month to make that. And that will never leave me.'

Graeme wandered into the room. He hasn't had the same pop-starry attention focused on him and, being a cynic, is fine with that. But you get the impression that he wants people to appreciate him for his talent. After all, he is the main music force of the band. He writes the songs and he's the boss in the sudio. Wet Wet Wet is his band, which he created and shaped over the years. However, he would also

OPPOSITE
Marti in concert, 1993

be the first to admit that the champagne lifestyle is easy to slip into. 'I've always had a live-for-the-day lifestyle,' he said, shaking his head, 'and I think in the short term.' He revealed he once lost four thousand pounds in a Mexican hotel, shrugged his shoulders and said, '*Que sera*.' 'That doesn't mean I take it all for granted,' he said. 'I haven't forgotten I used to get thirty pounds a fortnight on the dole. But I like to enjoy myself.'

He does. The clothes, the parties – he's a man who likes to squeeze the most out of a day. Even when there's nothing left. Hollywood legend Steve McQueen used to order two steaks every time he went to a restaurant, just so he could remind himself he could now afford the luxury of being able to eat what he liked. Graeme has some of that. 'People say to me that I've changed in the past ten years,' he said, 'and I say "Of course I've changed! Haven't you?".' At this point in the conversation, Graeme sighed and revealed that changes in his life meant the free-and-easy days were never going to be quite the same again. He was, in fact, a father. His girlfriend, Beverly, had given birth a few weeks earlier to a baby boy named Alexander. 'There you go, an exclusive for you,' he said, almost breathing a sigh of relief. 'He's just incredible. And that's why I'm even starting to think about pensions and whatever.' He paused. 'Well, sort of.'

Graeme may not be the most financially astute member of the band, but he is more than aware of his own strengths. 'Graeme is one of the best producers in the business,' said Elliot. 'If all this collapsed tomorrow he would make a good living in the studio. He has an instinctive ear for what's right. And as the Wets have grown, so has his ability.'

Most people in the business would agree Graeme is the musical force in the band. Their songwriting is more or less a team effort and each member brings ideas along to a session – but it's Graeme who pulls it all together. And he's not completely naïve about the vagaries of the music business. 'We're lucky; we just re-signed a publishing deal with Chrysalis for a lot of money, which sort of secures us,' he said. 'The managing director actually came to Glasgow to meet us. It's only fair. They signed us for buttons eight years ago, but then last year we went back to them with a number-one single and then the album. It put us in the driving seat. Now, the money gives you a nice feeling. It alleviates a lot of pressure.'

Neil, on the other hand, is one of those guys who seems to carry the weight of the world on his shoulders. He doesn't say too much, but it's not because he doesn't think about issues. He simply feels his opinions aren't important enough to shout about and recognises the world doesn't spin round him. He undervalues himself. In conversation, Neil gives the impression he landed the job with Wet Wet Wet under false pretences. He often puts himself down as a musician, although the others in the band would always say he more than pulls his weight. But that's Neil. He couldn't get carried away if you nailed his backside to a sedan chair. 'I don't go with all the success thing,' he said. 'And, as I've said before, I don't think I'm a great performer or a great player. I hide behind the keyboards on stage, and being in front of ten thousand people is all a bit strange for me. I'm not good at dealing with all this attention. Even in interviews like this I don't know what I'm expected to say. It's been hard for me because I'm basically my own person. I don't really have much of a social life. I keep to myself and I don't go to clubs. My

problem is doing videos or doing the press. The other guys are better at that sort of thing.'

He had a steady girlfriend and by this time was living in a fantastic flat in Glasgow's trendy West End, next to Graeme. 'It's great to be able to see the world and enjoy the benefits of the business. But I've still got the worry about making the next album good and thinking this could all end tomorrow. That's just me, I guess.'

Elliot warned me not to be fooled into thinking the boys were as unaffected as they appeared. 'They may play football and drink in the local pubs,' he said, laughing, 'but they don't forget for a minute they're famous. You can't push them around.'

And why shouldn't they be accorded star status? They've generated the income of a third-world country and spend most of it in Scotland. At the same time they're not adverse to giving something

back. In May 1993 the album and video *Live at the Royal Albert Hall* were released for Nordoff Robbins. The album made it to number ten. 'It's not just about money either,' said Neil. 'It's about encouraging kids to have fun.' That was a huge success, but the Wets had to concentrate on their next album. It was to be crucial to their careers. They were *still* looking for that new mature sound that could do for them what *Faith* and *Listen Without Prejudice* had done for George Michael.

In August, Graeme and Marti set off for New York to talk with a top record producer. The plan was for the band to work with the legendary Nile Rodgers on three tracks for their next album, at his famous Hit Factory studios. Rodgers had already launched the recording career of Madonna and worked with '70s dance sensations Chic and, later on, David Bowie. 'We are planning a major assault on the States in the New Year,' announced Elliot. 'And, hopefully, Rodgers will open some doors for us. He has tremendous connections with radio stations and we've had a huge difficulty in the past being playlisted. They simply don't have a category for the Wets' music. But, hopefully, the Rodgers link will help with all of that.'

At first, all went well. Marti and Graeme flew to meet Rodgers in Manhattan, were picked up in a limo and had breakfast with the recording legend. The Wets' advance party liked what they heard. It seemed that Rodgers would earn the reported £50,000 he was to bank up for sprinkling his magic dust on new tracks 'Shed a Tear' and 'Cold Cold Heart'. But it didn't turn out that way at all. Six weeks later, sitting in their management office in Glasgow, Tommy and Graeme were to argue that, in their eyes, the god of production had proved to be mortal. 'We thought he would do wonders, but I don't know that he did that much,' said Tommy. 'He didn't add as much sparkle as I expected.'

Graeme was less magnanimous. 'That was a complete and utter waste of money,' he said. 'All Rodgers did was fill a tin full of dried beans and shake it during the recording of "Cold Cold Heart". We could have produced the song better on our own. We learned absolutely nothing.' Elliot later admitted Graeme had said from day one that the Rodgers plan was doomed.

'Shed a Tear', very much a Little Feat derivative, only made number twenty-two in the charts. And 'Cold Cold Heart', arguably as good as anything George Michael had produced on *Faith*, failed to make a real dent in the charts, barely scratching the Top Twenty.

The next plan, however, did work. The idea was that the Wets would become the first band ever to sponsor a football team. Their local team, Clydebank, were to be kitted out with the words 'Wet Wet Wet' emblazoned across their chests, and the idea was that not only football fans would buy the shirts, but Wets fans would buy them at concerts. The sponsorship also extended to all forms of club merchandise. It worked. Advance orders for the shirts outstripped all orders for the previous season. It didn't really matter if the Wets were, in fact, Rangers fans first and foremost. They still had a soft spot for the Bankies and proved it by showing up at their home games. Part of the deal was that the band be given an executive box, where family and friends could come along and watch the game. Marti's and Tommy's dads were in heaven. Football continued to play an important part in the band's lives. When U2 announced a Parkhead concert, the Wets challenged them to a game – and won.

But in the charts the band were still failing to score. Two failed

singles didn't particularly bother them, but they seemed to have a problem in getting down to writing enough quality material to choose from. It had been almost two years since *High on the Happy Side* was released. And it would be another eighteen months before the next album came out. They were good songwriters but they weren't prolific. For the first time, the band's solidarity looked like being seriously challenged. Glasgow's *Evening Times* produced a story that was to set the pop world talking. Marti had auditioned for the lead role in a West End production of The Who's rock musical, *Tommy*. Top producer Cameron Mackintosh, who had earlier considered Marti for the lead in *Miss Saigon*, called the Wets' office to

talk about it; he was looking for a young charismatic pop star who could sing and, clearly, Marti fitted the bill. That in itself wasn't a great surprise. After all, Marti had had offers from everything from *Neighbours* to Hollywood movies. But the difference this time was that he said he was definitely interested. Marti had been a fan of The Who since he was a boy. 'This is one of the few stage roles I'd even consider,' he said. 'When you are offered the lead role in *Tommy*, that's something you have to seriously think about. And Roger Daltrey is one of my all-time heroes.'

But the rest of the band were stunned when they read the story in the paper. 'That was the first I knew of it,' said Tommy. 'And the first thing you think is "What does this mean for the band?".'

It was to be the beginning of several solo projects Marti was to consider. In August that year he was asked to do an advertisement for Head and Shoulders shampoo. This, of course, would have been a real break of policy for the band, who had previously never even considered lending their name – or their hair – to any product.

Marti was interested – at first. 'It turns out they did a survey of young women on who they would like to see in the ad, and my name kept cropping up,' he said. 'If they offer you a ridiculous amount of money, you'd be daft not to take it.' But later he changed his mind. 'It was flattering to be asked, you know, and then I found out they do animal testing. Of course, we as a band are heavily into the abolition of that, so I told them to stuff it up their arse.' He touched his hair and laughed. 'And just look at its condition now! All split ends and everything.'

The band could well afford to turn down the Head and Shoulders people. In August, while playing in the States, Marti revealed he had a curry sent over from Glasgow, picked up at JFK airport and whisked to the boys. At over a grand, it was probably the most expensive chicken tikka in the world.

But while the tales of pop-star excess were being tabloided, *The News of the World* were delving back into the pre-fame days. Tommy admitted in an article that he'd used drugs. 'I was unemployed when I left Clydebank High School,' he said. 'There were drugs everywhere and I got involved. I was rehearsing with the band and smoking too much dope at the same time. But I got into a huge depression and came close to a nervous breakdown. I felt like a bum. All my friends were laughing, saying, "So, you think you're going to be a big pop star?" It was the lowest point of my life and drugs dragged me down.'

Marti's admission was also something of a shocker – especially to his mum. He told how he'd been offered a role in an 'art house' movie, and that same month it was revealed that while in Amsterdam with Nile Rodgers the lads had 'lived it up in a sex club'. 'This was all nonsense,' say the Wets, 'but not worth suing over.'

Meanwhile, BBC Scotland were announcing a TV new drama that was to have the Wets' tongues wagging. *Down Among the Big Boys* starred Scots comedy giant Billy Connolly and it contained some lines referring to the band. And they were far from complimentary. In the programme, Connolly's screen character, JoJo Donnelly, came home one night to discover his wife and daughter singing along to 'Goodnight Girl'. 'What's that rubbish?' says JoJo. 'Wet Wet Wet,' replies his wife. 'Wet Wet Wet? More like pish, pish pish,' retorts JoJo. 'I wouldn't open the curtains to watch them if they were playing in the back garden.'

The reason for the vitriol? At the Nelson Mandela concert in

1988, Marti and Billy met backstage, while the singer was still running on adrenaline from performing the show. Marti then had a go at Billy, claiming the comedian had turned his back on Scotland and that he'd criticised the Wets home town of Clydebank. Sure enough, heavy words were exchanged.

People talking of the incident now say it's fortunate for the Wets star that Billy Connolly had given up alcohol and developed a new inner calm. 'He felt like killing Marti that night,' reported a Glasgow actor. 'And a few years back he would have done so without even blinking. Marti Pellow can count his blessings.'

Connolly's revenge was more subtle, having his writer pal, Peter McDougall, craft a few lines to the *Big Boys* script.

'Marti has poor recollection of the events of that night,' said Elliot, 'but he feels it was a storm in a teacup and makes it clear that he bears no hard feelings towards Billy Connolly for the situation which developed.'

The band, except Marti, were shaken again in November when a story in *The Evening Times* said the singer was being lined up to replace Craig MacLachlan in the West End production of *Grease*. Marti was once again interested, but the official line from a pragmatic Elliot at Precious was that it depended upon the band's commitments. Marti was keeping faith with his buddies but he wasn't saying no. And why should he? After six years the Wets knew they had outlasted most pop bands of their day. And although they had amazing self-belief, they could never tell how long the public or their record company would stay faithful.

Meanwhile, on the road, the Wets' large-scale UK tour was a sell-out. Were the boys happy? 'They're never entirely happy,' said Elliot.

'They would be much happier if the music press were giving them a new respect. They'd be happy if they could break America. But then, maybe not being happy is what keeps them going.'

In late November, Elliot, in a matter-of-fact conversation, revealed a 'little bit of news' that was to affect the Wets' entire career. A small British film production company had offered them the chance to take part in a low-budget project by recording a cover song for the soundtrack. 'I've told them we'll probably do it,' said the manager. 'I don't know the song yet, but at least it's nice to be asked.'

It was more than 'nice'. The offer would make Wet Wet Wet millionaires. It was film director Mike Newell who was anxious to secure the services of the band for a new film he was making. The title? *Four Weddings and a Funeral*. Of course, this offer meant nothing to the band at the time. What was keeping them going was the release of *End of Part One –Their Greatest Hits*, which reached number four. It was given this title because the band wanted everyone to know they still had a long way to go. Ironically, the Wets were to become one of the most successful bands in the world in 1994. But not for the reason they would have liked.

Chapter Ten

Love is All Around

WET WET WET were still brooding over 'Cold Cold Heart' at the start of 1994. After all, it had been a class song, one which should have had people taking them seriously. A lot depended on it, not just retrieving the money poured into buying some of Nile Rodgers' magic dust, but it was hoped the track would help them break America. 'We were hoping this song would take us into the clubs and give us credibility,' said Elliot. 'And we were hoping Nile Rodgers' credibility in America would have helped with radio airplay. We needed a leg up. But it didn't happen.'

It was time for a back-to-basics, softer approach for the band, which they had worked out in 1991. This was reflected in the way the band were being publicised. Elliot was going for a more pragmatic, relaxed, low-key approach where newspaper interviews were limited and the band instead agreed to be profiled in the serious magazines. Probably for the first time, Elliot reckoned it now didn't matter if Marti's was the only face on the front cover.

The back-to-bacics notion certainly applied to the band's forthcoming month-long tour of Europe, the 'cheese-and-ham toastie tour' they called it, referring to the fact it was not a flashy, expensive, hired-jet tour of the major cities. Instead, the band travelled by bus. It was a great success. As usual, the Wets had no problems in winning over a live audience.

Back in Britain, though, fate was taking a hand in the Wets' future. Down in Phonogram studios their A&R man, Alan Pell, was selecting songs for the movie *Four Weddings and a Funeral* which Phonogram were also to distribute. 'The film people have been on again,' Elliot told the band. 'I don't know too much about the movie, but we'll have a go.'

PREVIOUS PAGE
With Reg Presley,
writer of 'Love is All
Around'

The band were given a choice of only three songs and it came down to a final selection between a Barry Manilow song, 'Could It Be Magic?', and The Troggs' 1967 Top Ten hit, 'Love is All Around'. All the band – except one – agreed that the best of a bad bunch was The Troggs' number. 'No offence to Mr Manilow, but the voting between me and the group was four to one for the other song,' announced Elliot some months later. 'And no, I won't tell you who voted against it!'

In fact, it was Marti. Elliot, of course, was trying to spare his lead singer the sniggers. Thankfully, the rest of the band would have nothing to do with the Manilow cover. This was the year of credibility, for God's sake. So, the band went into their own recording studios in the New Year at the Brill Building in the centre of Glasgow, and a day later they came out with the recording that was to blow the record-buying world apart. Of course, at this point, the band had no idea that they'd produced an incredible recording. 'We've been given an old Troggs number to tinker around with,' said one of the band, 'and we've had a bit of fun with it. Yeah, it sounds okay, but it's not really our type of music. It's not the sort of cover we'd normally do.'

A few weeks later the film was released and became a huge international success. So did the single. *Melody Maker* loved it. 'Magnificent, gorgeous, sumptuous,' they said, changing their earlier stance. Everything was right about the song. The mood of the times was retro and this '60s sound was perfect for a 'summer of love'. Even the situation in Northern Ireland looked to be heading for peace. But as 'Love is All Around' shot up the charts, the Wets had mixed reactions. Sure, they were delighted to see a song they had produced in Glasgow being so well received. But the problem was, it wasn't their song. They weren't even fans of The Troggs. 'If we'd had to dip into

the 1960s and pick a song, it wouldn't have been this one,' said Elliot. 'It would have been something with a bit more credibility.'

But the band gradually changed their tune when the song sold in enormous quantities. Not only did it stay at number one in Britain but it began to sell in huge numbers across the world, reaching the top of the charts in fourteen countries. The irony of all this wasn't lost on the Wets. Here they were in 1994 planning to stick to producing serious music and becoming virtual recluses. Yet suddenly they were responsible for the most popular song of the decade. They had to go with the flow, of course, and on 12 May, at the London première of *Four Weddings*, the Wets fully entered the spirit of the occasion and kilted up. Their star was clearly in the ascendant. Even Graeme's snooker was at its best when he was narrowly beaten by Jimmy White in a charity match, raising £6,000 for Nordoff Robbins Music Therapy.

In June, Marti was back in the minds of movie producers and was offered a role in Ken Russell's film, *Boadicea*. He was asked to play a woad-covered warrior but Elliot suspected the singer's name would be used simply to generate investors' money. Elliot played call-my-bluff and asked for starter-money up-front, something around £100,000. Nothing appeared, and the manager laughed about the 'amateurism' of the film outfit.

But it did illustrate the demand for Marti, which continued as the single stayed at the number-one spot. Yet the song's success, surprisingly, didn't mean that the boys made big bucks. Because Reg Presley wrote the song, he received mechanical royalties from sales. And each time the song was played on air, all of the Performing Rights Society money went to Reg. It's no wonder the Troggs frontman, who was still working the '60s revival circuit, was happy.

PREVIOUS PAGE
*Wet Wet Wet
working hard on the
promotion trail*

In June, *The Evening Times* drove Reg from Edinburgh to meet the band for the first time. It was quite an occasion. The Wets were rehearsing in a theatre venue in the city centre for upcoming British tour dates. 'I just love the Wets' version of the song,' said Reg, by now in his fifties, in his Wurzelish accent. 'When I heard the first screaming chord I thought, "Oh my God," but then that acoustic guitar came in and it all sounded wonderful.'

Although the Wets were never Troggs fans, they took to the ebullient Reg immediately. 'You're a survivor, Reg,' declared Tommy. And he was.

'I've been good to you boys, with this song,' said Reg, grinning.

'Not half as good as we've been to you, Reg,' replied Tommy.

When the Wets asked him to sing 'Love is All Around' Reg was a little choked. He sang the song, not quite in his key, and the Wets replied with generous applause. They talked for a while and Graeme, Tommy, Neil and Graeme Duffin quizzed the singer about his tours in the 1960s with the likes of The Who. But then Marti arrived, looking tanned and fit in a denim shirt and jeans, and paid tribute to old Reg in the best way possible. 'This one's for you, Reg,' said the young pretender.

And when Marti began to sing Presley's eyes filled up with tears. 'That fella's got the best pop voice I've ever heard,' he said. 'Don't he play that just wonderfully.' Well, yes, Reg. The Canadians, Dutch, Australians, even the Guatemalans agreed. And as a result, Wet Wet Wet became the most sought-after band in Europe for press interviews. But they stayed almost silent, surfacing only occasionally to deny rumours like the one in July which suggested the band would be asked to record the title song for the next Bond film. It's news to me, said

Elliot – but then at this point anything was possible.

But a little glitch was to appear in the smooth workings of the Wets' PR machine. Marti's personal life again hit the headlines in August when reports suggested his romance with Eileen Catterson was on the rocks, when it was alleged, in a piece of nonsense, that he had banned her from his Helensburgh home. It was also claimed he had refused to marry her. He hadn't, of course, 'banned' her from his home – they were still very much together. A source close to Eileen said Marti had asked his girlfriend to move in, and had asked her to marry him. It was argued, said Eileen's friend, that she had refused because she valued her independence. In the other camp, Marti was saying nothing. A couple of weeks later, Eileen was to give Marti a real scare. She was hit by a mystery virus and spent some time in hospital, though was declared well a few weeks later.

Meanwhile, 'Love is All Around' continued to dominate the British and European charts. More importantly for the band, in cash terms, sales of their *End of Part One* album went through the roof. The band had simultaneous number-one single and album success in Britain, Denmark, The Netherlands, New Zealand, Eire, Germany and Sweden.

Even John Finch rode to fame on the back of the Wets. He was television's *Stars in Your Eyes* Marti Pellow lookalike who won the grand finale singing 'Goodnight Girl'. He didn't know it at the time but the Wets were all rooting for him. 'All the boys and their families were phoning in to make sure he won,' said Elliot. 'We thought it was absolutely brilliant.'

But as 'Love is All Around' was nearing fifteen weeks in the charts, the band were said to be bored to tears with the hit song. Nevertheless, they wanted to beat the British sales records. They were a week away from Bryan Adams' record of sixteen weeks at the top with 'Everything I Do' in 1991. That had also been a soundtrack single. However, on week fifteen it looked as though sales were dropping dramatically. But Elliot came up with a stunt that he hoped would put his band in the record books. The plan was to announce the song would be deleted at the end of the week. The reason given was that the band wanted to clear the charts for their next record release. This was pure nonsense of course. Elliot's clever scheme was to jolt potential record buyers into thinking this was their last chance at the song – and thus create a surge of demand. On Radio 1 that week Mark Goodier did announce the band were to delete the song but he smelled a rat and laughed as he

Marti's former home in Helensburgh

said it. Reg Presley didn't, though. He'd heard 'Love is All Around' was to be deleted and, instead of thinking, his mouth opened up – to *The Sun*. 'Marti is a madman,' he was quoted as saying. 'I'm going to get him a good psychiatrist. He needs his head looking into.' That was rich coming from a man who spends his cash on investigating crop circles. 'I want the record to stay in the charts,' said Reg. 'Every time it's played on Radio I make money.' Sure, but the Wets didn't, Reg.

The Sun said Reg was threatening to sue. He argued that the band had had to ask his permission to release the record, and that they should have to ask for it to be deleted. Presley had earned over a million pounds from the song. And, unlike the Wets, he didn't have to cut his cash five ways. It seemed he didn't see through the deletion scam – maybe he'd been spending too long investigating the visits of aliens.

Ironically, the 'Reg in Raging Anger' story was also a nice bit of hype which helped sales – but sadly not enough, because the ploy failed. The following week, a previously unknown Scandinavian singer, Whigfield, was to knock the Wets off the number-one spot with 'Saturday Night', a piece of Eurodisco dance nonsense. Still, the Wets' disappointment was cushioned by the fact that they were really fed up with the song; they hadn't written it, and it had taken their image off in the wrong direction. But it had also made them incredibly popular. And there was a change in Phonogram's attitude; the band were declared a top international priority by the record company.

They took off on a series off European concerts: Vienna, Cologne, Frankfurt, Amsterdam and Stockholm. Then it was off to Sydney, Melbourne and Brisbane before embarking on an American tour at the end of August, often playing live on American radio. Elliot insisted on that, because, simply put, it was what they did best. The band's big problem in the States still remained, however. American radio was highly formatted and programme controllers couldn't easily pigeon-hole the 'blue-eyed soul' of the band. 'We're all over the shop,' said Marti, nicely summing up the band's American position.

The singer's heart wasn't entirely in the PR side of tour. On one occasion, in Texas, a band insider revealed Marti was so fed up doing radio interviews that Tommy had to pretend he was the lead singer and do the interviews instead. Marti, at this point, had gone moody. If he was up for a promotional idea, he'd do it. If not, it would be easier to move the Catskill mountains. In November, *The Sun* ran a story saying Marti was fed up with 'the pop-star bit'. In turned out he'd been offered the lead role in Andrew Lloyd Webber's hit show *Jesus Christ Superstar*. They quoted a band insider who said that 'Love is All Around' had 'made the band millionaires but Marti just doesn't want to do all the touring and promoting that goes with another world tour'. Well, given the Texas story, that seemed to be about right. Since he was nineteen, Marti had known nothing but writing and touring. The Wets had only produced four albums of original material, but they had played America, Australia and Europe and toured the world. Marti was now twenty-nine. He had known nothing of adult life outside of being a pop star and it was understandable that he might now be keen to try something that didn't involve the band – but not at the expense of destroying all that had been built up over the years.

'Yes, he'd love to go on stage,' confirmed Elliot. 'It would be a whole new challenge for him. But *The Sun* story about him being totally fed up is untrue. We'd sue, but what the hell good would it do?'

Marti was clearly going through a difficult phase. In August, *The*

Sun revealed that his older brother, John, was a hopeless alcoholic. And later, when the same paper were sold sneaky photographs taken inside the singer's Helensburgh home while he was off touring, he blew his top. 'I feel as if I've been raped,' he said. He was so distraught he immediately announced he would sell his house. Sure enough, the next week it was on the market and Marti was seen checking out the top end of the Glasgow property scene. 'He's actually talking about moving to Amsterdam,' said a close friend. 'He loves it there and he's had enough of being subjected to harsh personal intrusion in his home town.'

Marti didn't go to Amsterdam, but he did take off to the States in October to revisit Memphis. The Wets were the only British band invited to appear at 'Elvis Aaron Presley – The Tribute', a concert sanctioned by the Presley estate and hosted by Priscilla Presley. Elliot, it turns out, had almost gate-crashed the party. 'I was sitting in the New York office of the president of Island Records who was talking with John Reid, Elton's manager, and I overheard that Elton was supposed to be doing the show, so I suggested very strongly that the Wets should also do it. There was no chance.'

But after many long-distance phone calls from Elliot, the UK chairman of Polygram agreed. The Wets appeared on stage on 8 October with the likes of Jerry Lee Lewis, Iggy Pop, Bryan Adams and Tony Bennett. And the Glasgow boys blew the rest of the acts away, playing 'It's Now or Never'. The legendary Sam Moore said Marti was the best singer on the night. Such was the strength of their performance of 'It's Now or Never', the Wets were 'begged' to record the song as a track on an album, to commemorate – or cash in on – the evening, and then to release it as a single. The Wets turned down the idea of the single. It was a tremendous risk to take – turning down a clear chart opportunity in the States which the band had dreamed of for so long. The reason? 'Love is All Around'. They reckoned that a recording of another cover version was exactly what the band didn't need at this time. 'We want to remind people we can write our own material,' they said. 'And we have a song written called "Julia Says" coming out in the spring. We want that to be the Wets' next big hit.'

Memphis was, of course, the home of Willie Mitchell, their old producer pal who had worked with them on the *Memphis Sessions* back in 1986. After the Elvis show, the band made the pilgrimage to his house. Willie wasn't home.

Clearly, in financial terms, the year had been a huge success. In December the band announced they'd be staging a 23-date tour of Britain, and a tour of Europe. Six nights in Glasgow at the 10,000-seater SECC were sold out in days and the band would gross more than a million pounds from their sell-out concert dates in that city alone.

But the year hadn't gone to plan. The idea of keeping a low profile and being taken seriously had evaporated. Of course, no one could have predicted the success of 'Love is All Around'. But the band didn't stick to their gameplan of keeping out of the tabloids and seeking musical maturity. In November, Marti played the game he'd decried for years. He did the *Hello!* magazine photoshoot, after Elliot spent some months haggling over money, first offering *The Sun* a deal and then the glossy, through-the-keyhole mag. Initially, *Hello!* had cheekily asked for the photos for free, saying it would be good prestige for the boys, and then offered five grand. But, when Elliot did the deal after 'Love is All Around' had been in the charts for four months, the price was quite a bit more.

Chapter Eleven

Picture This

AFTER THE Christmas holiday break, the band were back in the studio writing songs for the forthcoming album, *Picture This*. The Wets had already selected the next single, 'Julia Says', a perky song so John Lennon-like you could almost hear Yoko in the background calling the copyright lawyer. 'It's an all-important song,' said Elliot, not exaggerating in the slightest. 'It *has* to make the Top Ten.' He was right. The Wets hadn't had a Top Ten hit they'd written themselves since 'Goodnight Girl' – three years previously.

Marti, meantime, was occupied with finding a new home. In the second week of January he suffered a major disappointment when he

Elliot Davis hosts an art party at the Brill Building, Glasgow, 1994

180

lost out in a bid to buy the famous 'Greek' Thompson House, an 'A' listed building in Glasgow's prestigious Great Western Terrace, a house which was said to cost more than three hundred grand.

But it wasn't all winter blues. There came a surprise delight when it was announced that the famous Italian tenor, Luciano Pavarotti, would love to duet with Wet Wet Wet's frontman. 'Wow!' said Marti. 'Pavarotti wants to sing with *me*!' Big Pav invited the band to perform at his annual concert in Modena and they said, 'Sure – provided you perform with us at the Brits pop awards ceremony.'

But the Brits performance in March never came about, because the Wets themselves were not asked to appear alongside the likes of Elton and Prince. 'It's an absolute disgrace,' said Elliot, echoing comments he had made two years earlier, and angry that the band had lost out on a chance to showcase the new single. 'We had the biggest-selling single in Europe last year and we weren't even asked to perform live. The excuse we were given was that the names had all been drawn up. But even when some people withdrew we were never included. And who are the likes of Eternal or Blur? Bloody novelty acts compared to the Wets, who've had constant chart success since 1987. Is there a hidden agenda?'

It was a difficult time for the mercurial manager. 'Julia Says' was set for release but immediately there were problems. When Radio 1 were given the first airplays, commercial radio stations in Scotland came down heavily on the manager. Arguments followed between Elliot and the bosses of one station, Radio Forth in Edinburgh, who then claimed they wouldn't play the single at all because of Elliot's attitude. The manager hit back, saying this was part of the Scottish disease: the Scots don't honour their own success stories. He pointed

out that 'Julia Says' had been given priority placings in at least ten major independent radio stations in England – but it couldn't make the 'A' list in Central Scotland. 'These people have done nothing to help the Wets,' complained Elliot.

The single went to number three, so he needn't have worried. But the manager ran into more trouble with his pop art exhibition. The plan was to have leading Scottish artists paint members of the band and to exhibit the finished works around the major cities of Europe to coincide with the band's appearances there, as well as using them to illustrate the new album. Great plan, especially since one of the paintings was a nude study of Marti Pellow. But there were mumblings of discontent when *The Sunday Times* ran an article before the Glasgow exhibition in March, saying that several of the artists were so unhappy that they were threatening an injunction. But the flipside of this was the artists' work was displayed all over Europe. And no artist actually complained. In fact, John Byrne, whose brilliant illustration featured on the front of *Picture This*, was said to be 'delighted'.

To publicise the new album, which was to shoot to number one in the charts, the band didn't do the tabloid interviews; instead, they stuck to glossy men's mags such as *Loaded*. Marti spoke of dealing with the public's attentions: 'The whole idea of sex symbols has always struck me as a bit ridiculous,' he said. 'They say Sean Connery is the sexiest man in Europe. But when you get right down to it, he's a sixty-five-year-old Scottish baldy bastard. If he worked on a building site he'd just be Baldy Sean and women wouldn't give him a second glance. But because he's a famous film star, he gets the sex symbol treatment. I'm sure it's the same with me. If I worked in a

PREVIOUS PAGES
Neil Mitchell and
Graeme Clark at the
Picture This art party,
1995

bank, I wouldn't get the same attention. If anything with me, it all seems to be about the smile.'

What about those teeth, Marti?, asked the interviewer. 'Yeah, they're all mine, all bought and paid for and handcrafted by a top team of cosmetic dentists. Cost a fortune but they're worth every penny. After all, they made me the sex symbol I am.'

It was good to see the singer throw out a nice line in irony. But the *Loaded* interview was more interesting perhaps for what *didn't* appear in print – it brought home the internal rift in the band. The publishers had, in fact, offered Elliot the front cover – provided it was a solo photo of Marti. So, too, did other glossy mags. Elliot, unusually, suggested Marti do them, even though for years he'd demanded the band should always be pictured together for magazine or newspaper interviews. The manager was being pragmatic. He reckoned the band had now managed to cross over from being seen as a teeny band and become a mainstream act and, as such, had nothing to fear from Marti being featured; after all, it was his face everyone wanted to see anyway.

But Tommy and Graeme didn't see it that way. Continually bugged by stories in the papers over the years about Marti being offered a solo career and Marti being the Wets, the magazine solo shots, for them, represented the beginning of the end for the band.

Ironically, Marti wasn't happy either about stepping outside the normal four-way photo plan. It's one thing being tempted by the offer to star in the West End or to think about taking a sabbatical, but it's another to be seen to be acting The Star. To use an old Scots football line, Marti would have been selling the jerseys.

Tommy and Graeme, of course, have valid arguments as to why

the band shouldn't be Marti Pellow and The Wets. Sure, Graeme often likes to act out the role of pop star to the full, but he is the band's major musical force; and it's no coincidence that he's now standing up to be counted as such by demanding a producer credit on the new album, alongside another forgotten man in the band, Graeme Duffin.

Tommy too has his plans. As well as having a great ear for music, he is in many ways the band's backbone, the spokesman, the voice of common sense. And that's not to ignore the importance of Neil. Other musicians rate him a very good keyboard player and Elliot always maintains that his piano flourishes go a long way to breathing life into the Wets' songs. And the fact that Neil is easy-going, goes with the flow and has no discernible ego is crucial. No band can survive with four competing egos. Neil's unaffected approach to the pop business sets a positive tone within the band.

But Elliot and the band are clearly five individuals moving forward. And there are questions about their future, indicated by the album credits. If Graeme lands a producer's fee, what about the writing credits? He does most of the writing, with contributions from Marti and Neil, but Tommy doesn't really write. And in terms of solo appearance money, Marti could blow the rest away. He is the one who's wanted for theatre and film roles. Should the band sanction a short-term split? In the past it was very much a 'one for all and all for one' attitude, but now the democratic structure of the band is under strain. And what if Graeme Duffin formally joins the band?

PREVIOUS PAGES
Marti at the Picture This Art Party, Glasgow City Chambers, 1995

Drummer Tommy Cunningham, 1993

Whatever the internal conflicts, which have bubbled under the surface for ten years, it's certain the Wets will survive as a band. There are two reasons for this. The first is that they genuinely are friends and each would be lost without the others. 'The record business is full of five-furlong bands,' says Derek Chalmers, who recorded that first-ever demo. 'And the Wets are certainly three-milers. The reason is because they're four mates who fit together. And they haven't developed the egos a lot of people in this business suffer from. I met Graeme a couple of months ago and, being a bass-player myself, we got to talking about new guitars. I recommended one in particular and he stunned me when he replied, "Yes, they're great – but they're too expensive." He could have bought the factory!'

Secondly, the band still face a battle which they are determined to win – to prove themselves to the public, to show they can occupy the hallowed ground of adult respectability which former teen idol George Michael enjoys. 'We always wanted to be something more than the housewives' choice or the teeny-boppers' favourites,' said Marti recently. 'Suddenly we were perceived as this teeny-bop band and we were never comfortable with that. The whole *Smash Hits* thing quickly became an albatross around our neck. We became the sort of band whose posters were pinned to little girls' bedroom walls and I wouldn't wish that on my worst enemy. Thankfully, the whole teeny-bop thing seems to have gone away right now. The success of "Love is All Around" has opened our audience right up again.' And it has continued with 'Don't Want to Forgive Me Now' hitting the Top Ten in June.

But Wet Wet Wet are four changing individuals. And it seems odds-on that Marti will go his own way in some form, perhaps take a sabbatical to appear in a movie or a musical. He's keen and he certainly has the talent, with one of the best pop voices on the planet and an on-stage charisma most performers would kill for. The need to go solo has nothing to do with money. By the summer of '95 the band were all millionaires and a new record-company deal was thrashed out which would set them up for life. But aged thirty, he's keen for fresh challenges.

However, it is certain the band will survive as long as they continue to write good pop songs. And they've shown they have the longevity to last ten years in an incredibly fickle business. When the Clydebank four first hit the charts they were up against the likes of Curiosity, The Blow Monkeys, The Christians, Level 42, Boy George and Fine Young Cannibals. Enough said?

They've had their lucky breaks, sure. 'Goodnight Girl' breathed new life into their career when the public yawned. 'Love is All Around' gave them space to write new songs for the next album and the vehicle from which to launch an international concert tour which would again propel their name across the world.

Looking back, it's hard to tell if the Wets have made mistakes. Can you remain loyal to Scotland *and* become an international success? Have they paid the price for their parochiality? If they'd moved out of Glasgow, would they have thrived? Probably not. The city has given them common roots and a common goal – to live and work there successfully.

What is it that has made the band so successful? Andrea Miller believes the Wets would have been successful no matter what, but believes Elliot Davis is a top-notch manager in a cut-throat business. Could another manager have given them greater international success? The jury is out on that one. But Elliot would probably admit he's failed the Wets as far as the lack of American success goes.

However, Wet Wet Wet, as their manager has often said, can only

The band at the Picture This art exhibition in Glasgow, 1995

blow it for themselves. Together they form something special, they are a mutual support system. Like four walls of a room, take one away and the rest collapse.

It remains to be seen whether pop success will continue to change them to the point where their ambition dies and complacency sets in. Changes in their attitude, of course, are inevitable. You can't go from being dead-end kids from Clydebank to pop-star millionaires who've had seventeen hit singles and five hit albums and *not* be affected. But as the wealth and success grows, the danger is that they will lose sight of their old life, the Clydebank desperation, the dark school years, the reality of unemployment, the wasted lives all around them, all of which gave them the will to succeed in the first place.

Elliot admits that's the case. In one off-guard moment, clearly caught up in the frustration of dealing with one problem too many that day, he made a stark admission: 'I've lost track of where Marti's head lay since 1988. I haven't really known the Wets since then. And I'm never really sure of what these boys will do. But one thing's for sure: they have genuine talent, they write great pop songs – and they're survivors.'